World Class IT Service Delivery

The British Computer Society

BCS is the leading professional body for the IT industry. With members in over 100 countries, BCS is the professional and learned society in the field of computers and information systems.

BCS is responsible for setting standards for the IT profession. It is also leading the change in public perception and appreciation of the economic and social importance of professionally managed IT projects and programmes. In this capacity, the society advises, informs and persuades industry and government on successful IT implementation.

IT is affecting every part of our lives and that is why BCS is determined to promote IT as the profession of the 21st century.

Joining BCS

BCS qualifications, products and services are designed with your career plans in mind. We not only provide essential recognition through professional qualifications but also offer many other useful benefits to our members at every level.

BCS membership demonstrates your commitment to professional development. It helps to set you apart from other IT practitioners and provides industry recognition of your skills and experience. Employers and customers increasingly require proof of professional qualifications and competence. Professional membership confirms your competence and integrity and sets an independent standard that people can trust. Professional Membership (MBCS) is the pathway to Chartered IT Professional (CITP) Status.

www.bcs.org/membership

Further Information

Further information about BCS can be obtained from: BCS, First Floor, Block D, North Star House, North Star Avenue, Swindon SN2 1FA, UK.

Telephone: 0845 300 4417 (UK only) or + 44 (0)1793 417 424 (overseas)

Email: customerservice@hq.bcs.org.uk

Web: www.bcs.org

World Class IT Service Delivery

Peter Wheatcroft

Peter Wheatcroft

BCS

The British Computer Society
Publishing and Information Products
First Floor, Block D
North Star House
North Star Avenue
Swindon
SN2 1FA
UK

www.bcs.org

ISBN13 978-1-902505-82-4

British Cataloguing in Publication Data.
A CIP catalogue record for this book is available at the British Library.

All trademarks, registered names etc. acknowledged in this publication are to be the property of their respective owners.

Disclaimer:
The views expressed in this book are those of the author and do not necessarily reflect the views of the British Computer Society except where explicitly stated as such.

Although every care has been taken by the authors and the British Computer Society in the preparation of the publication, no warranty is given by the authors or the British Computer Society as publisher as to the accuracy or completeness of the information contained within it and neither the authors nor the British Computer Society shall be responsible or liable for any loss or damage whatsoever arising by virtue of such information or any instructions or advice contained within this publication or by any of the aforementioned.

 captured, authored, published, delivered and managed in XML
CAPDM Limited, Edinburgh, Scotland   **www.capdm.com**

Printed and bound in England by Antony Rowe Ltd, Chippenham, Wiltshire

Contents

Figures and tables

About the author

Peter Wheatcroft is a specialist in service transformation and has consulted widely in this area since 2002. He has recently been working with a large number of blue-chip companies to improve the management of their IT departments, leading to the establishment of flagship service standards in the UK, and these assignments have been the stimulus to write this book.

Before becoming independent, Peter was director of commercial and information management for Alliance & Leicester plc, where his responsibilities encompassed the business management of information services, including financial, supplier and technology partnerships and the attainment of world-class status for IT services and processes. Before that, he was the director of technology services responsible for integrating operational IT activities of the different group businesses – Alliance & Leicester, Girobank and Sovereign Finance – into a coherent unit that was externally benchmarked as 'best practice', including winning three Chartered Institute of Bankers (CIB) awards and commendations for technological achievement and also acknowledged by management, customers and staff. Until 1986, Peter was responsible for developing and delivering IT and IS services for the National Coal Board (NCB) South Yorkshire area.

He has a BSc in electrical and electronic engineering and is a chartered engineer and a chartered IT professional, holding fellowships from both the Institution of Engineering and Technology (IET) and the British Computer Society (BCS). He has been an active contributor to the Skills Framework for the Information Age (SFIA) and Industry Structure Model (ISM) career and skills development schemes for the BCS, and has refereed and subsequently judged the BCS IT Professional Awards since 2002. He is a member of the Chartered Management Institute and also a corporate member of the British Quality Foundation.

His papers and articles have been published in a number of trade journals such as *Service Talk, Computer Weekly, The Computer Bulletin, Support World, Biosmagazine, Computing Business* and *The Times*.

About the author

Acknowledgements

The author wishes to thank a number of people for their support in helping to write this book and their details are shown below.

All figures and tables are the work of the author except for the following:

Figure 1.1   Reproduced by kind permission of Professor Chris Voss from the London Business School.

Figure 2.3   Reproduced by kind permission of Amanda Koenig and Marc Wilkinson of HP.

Table 3.1   Reproduced by kind permission of the Skills for the Information Age (SFIA) Foundation.

Table 3.2   Data provided courtesy of the IS Examinations Board (ISEB).

Figure 4.4   Reproduced by kind permission of Cornelius Winkler Prins of Service Management Partners Inc.

Figure 6.2   Reproduced by permission of Paul Cash at Partners in IT Ltd.

Figure 6.3   Reproduced by permission of Laurel Quayle from Capita Group.

Figure 6.4   Reproduced by permission of Mark Ridsdale of Service Birmingham Ltd.

Figure 7.3   Produced by Simon Alison at Coffeehouse Digital.

Figure 8.1   Produced by Simon Alison at Coffeehouse Digital.

Figures 3.6 and 5.1 include original artwork produced by Joanna Wilde.

Permission to reproduce extracts of BS ISO/IEC 20000:2005 and BS ISO/IEC 17799:2005 is granted by BSI. British Standards can be obtained from BSI Customer Services, 389 Chiswick High Road, London W4 4AL; tel: +44 (0)20 8996 9001; email: cservices@bsi-global.com

Thanks are also extended to the following organizations, which have allowed extracts of their material to be used in this book. These organizations are: British Computer Society and, in particular, the ISEB and ECDL business units; London Business School; BSI; Intellect; SFIA Foundation; British Quality Foundation.

References to ITIL® material are covered by click-use licence C02W0005355 and it is acknowledged that ITIL® is a registered trade mark of Office of Government Commerce (OGC).

Alignability™ is a registered trade mark of Service Management Partners Inc and is used with permission.

Abbreviations

APM   Alignability Process Model

B2C   business to consumer

BCS   British Computer Society

BIA   business impact agreement

CI   configuration item

CIB   Chartered Institute of Bankers

CIO   chief information officer

CIS   customer information system

CITP   chartered IT professional

CMDB   configuration management database

CMMI   Capability Maturity Model Integration

CobiT   Control Objectives for Information Technology

CSF   critical success factor

CSR   corporate social responsibility

CTQ   critical to quality

DBA   database administrator

DCF   discounted cash flow

DMAIC   define, measure, analyse, improve and control

DR   disaster recovery

DRT   design review team

ECDL   European Computer Driving Licence

EFQM   European Foundation for Quality Management

ERP   enterprise resource planning

EXIN   Examination Institute for Information Science

FAST   Federation Against Software Theft

FMEA   failure modes and effect analysis

HR	human resources
ICT	information and communications technology
IET	Institution of Engineering and Technology
IP	intellectual property
IRR	internal rate of return
IS	information services
ISEB	IS Examinations Board
ISM	Industry Structure Model
ISMS	information security management system
ISO	International Organization for Standardization
ISP	internet service provider
ISQW	Information Systems Quality at Work
IT	information technology
ITGI	Information Technology Governance Institute
ITIL	Information Technology Infrastructure Library
ITSM	information technology service management
KPI	key performance indicator
LAN	local-area network
MIS	management information system
MOT	moment of truth
NPfIT	National Programme for information technology
NPV	net present value
ODI	organizational design indicator
OGC	Office of Government Commerce
OLA	operational level agreement
PC	personal computer
PDA	personal digital assistant
PIR	post-implementation review
QMS	quality management system
RFID	radio-frequency identification
ROI	return on investment

SCM	supply chain management
SFIA	Skills Framework for the Information Age
SIP	service improvement programme
SLA	service level agreement
SLM	service level management
SQI	service quality improvement
SSL	Secure Sockets Layer
TCO	total cost of ownership
VOC	voice of the customer
VoIP	Voice over Internet Protocol
VPN	virtual private network

Useful websites

Further information on the Glowinkowski approach to organizational development can be found at www.glowinkowski.com.

Information on the British Computer Society and its products, including details of the ISEB, ECDL, SFIA*plus*3, IT Professional Awards and ISQW initiatives, can be found at www.bcs.org.

Information about the MT/Unisys Service Excellence Awards can be found at www.serviceexcellenceawards.com.

Further information about the EFQM Excellence Model can be found at www.bqf.org.uk.

Information on ITIL® can be found from the OGC website at www.ogc.gov.uk.

Further information about Alignability™ can be found at www.alignability.com.

Information about CobiT can be found at www.itgi.com.

Details about the IT Service Management Forum can be found at www.itsmf.com.

Details about the Corporate Infrastructure Forum can be found at www.tif.co.uk.

Further details about INVEST can be obtained from Laurel Quayle at Capita Group on laurel.quayle@capita.co.uk.

Information on the capabilities of Coffeehouse Digital can be obtained from Simon Alison at www.coffeehousedigital.com.

Information on the Service Accession Model and other service management best practices can be found by contacting Partners in IT Ltd at www.piit.co.uk.

Intellect, the trade association for the IT, telecommunications and electronics industries in the UK, and its associated code of best practice can be referenced at www.intellectuk.org.

Information about the International Federation of the Recording Industry is at www.ifpi.org.

For more on TickIT, see www.tickit.org.

Information about the National Consumer Council is at www.ncc.org.uk.

Introduction

A backlash at shoddy customer service and unrelenting sales pitches is hitting British business where it hurts most – on the bottom line – warns a 2006 report from the National Consumer Council. 'The Stupid Company: How British businesses throw away money by alienating consumers' reveals a sorry picture of businesses over-promising and under-delivering, treating customers in a clinical and patronising way, and being incapable of getting the most basic things right. Too often they focus on making a quick profit at the expense of the longer-term relationship.

National Consumer Council

6 February 2006

Service is not a product. Unlike a manufactured article, service cannot be made by the thousand, pre-packaged and sold on at a discount. And also unlike a manufactured article, it cannot be stolen or disassociated from its creator. This is why service is a largely misunderstood part of the IT delivery chain. It is often confused with operations, derided as being the province of backroom staff, and yet it accounts for the greatest proportion of IT customer complaints when delivery does not match expectations. Of course, it could be argued that customer expectations might be wrong – but setting such aspirations in the first place is actually part of the IT service delivery cycle since, unlike its product counterpart, service *involves* the customer in the transaction. The 2006 report published by the National Consumer Council from which the above extract is taken explains just that.

Service delivery is more important now than at any time in the past, because not only is the IT environment getting more complex – with multiple technologies supporting each system – but the end-user has changed as well. As a supplier, IT has now become like the retail trade by providing services directly to the person in the street. And as any retailer knows only too well, the *service experience*, on which the customer will rate you, goes way beyond what is just being bought from you. Service intimately involves the person you are dealing with – it has become a highly cooperative transaction. So how should this affect how we manage IT services – and our customers?

This book explains why management of the customer is vital to both the actual and perceived success of overall IT service quality and guides the reader through the processes and techniques available to define and then deliver an appropriate level of IT service. Some readers will already have considered particular topics and have addressed the points raised – if so, this is commendable. The structure has been generated to allow the reader to concentrate on particular areas of interest, rather than like a novel, where you cannot read chapters out of sequence without spoiling the plot.

What became clear when this book was being written is how few companies in the UK have taken on board all the factors necessary to achieve consistent world-class service delivery. This is partly down to education and partly down to motivation – knowing what to do and then having the energy to do it. I hope that the contents will be of value to practitioners and their managers as well as anyone involved with training, planning or consultancy.

Peter Wheatcroft

1 Defining world class

The terms 'world class' and 'best practice' are often used interchangeably to describe the attainment level of a particular IT organization or service offering. However, they do not mean the same thing at all and it is important that the differences between these two terms are understood. This chapter defines 'world class' and 'best practice' as well as the relationship between them and then goes on to show how they can both be used to govern IT service delivery. A number of concepts and models are introduced, starting with some well-known examples from outside IT and concluding with an accession model developed by the author specifically for IT services departments.

WORLD CLASS VERSUS BEST PRACTICE

Imagine that you are a keen golfer. You have the opportunity to visit a variety of golf courses each month and so are developing a respectable handicap. Each course that you visit has defined the number of strokes that it will take a good golfer to get round in and this is universally known as par – as in the expression 'par for the course'. Terminology can get complicated here, since there can also be a standard scratch score defined for each course, but for the sake of simplicity this explanation will focus on par as meaning the expected standard of golfing achievement. Par for the course is the golfing equivalent of best practice and the measure of how much individual players differ from best practice is known as a handicap – so someone with a handicap of 16 would be expected to get round a par 80 course in 96 strokes in order to justify that handicap. The smaller the handicap, the better the player has to do in relation to the course par until the standard of achievement is such that he can get round exactly on par – having become a scratch golfer with a handicap of 0.

In the analogy above, a scratch player is achieving best practice as a golfer and you can see how this example can be interpreted in relation to IT service delivery. The gap between your current level of performance and the best-practice standards defined for service delivery is a handicap because it describes a shortfall in service quality and, just like in golf, this shortfall can be quantified by means of benchmarking, as explained in Chapters 3 and 8.

But the standards of service required for your organization may not be satisfied by best practice alone. Someone had to set par for the golf course you play on each month and this person can probably get round the course in even less than the defined number of strokes – and do so consistently. This expert has a positive handicap, which is used to rank their performance in competitions, where professional golfers usually play for high stakes. Getting round a course in less than the established par rating is the province of world-class golfers, and these are the people who define professionalism.

So world class sets the standards that govern best-practice developments. World class is the province of a defined elite that not only set the standards for others to follow but are consistently in competition with each other to produce ever higher levels of achievement, for which the winners get rewarded but the followers do not. This is the differentiator between IT service excellence and IT service good practice – just like the distinction between a professional and a leisure golfer. This is world-class IT in action.

INDUSTRY DEFINITIONS OF WORLD CLASS

World-class achievements are not just confined to golf, and neither are they an esoteric concept. The issues and characteristics of organizations that strive to achieve outstanding service performance can be analysed and measured, and a number of important models that do this are outlined in this chapter. But before looking at the models, it is useful to look at how world class has been defined more generally. For instance, the Government Accountability Office in the USA defines world-class organizations as being 'recognized as the best for at least one critical business process and are held as models for other organizations'. In contrast, The Bridgefield Group, which specializes in quality management and performance measurement systems, defines world class as being 'a general term for a high level of competitive performance as defined by benchmarking and use of best practices'. And not least of all, Wikipedia – an online collaborative encyclopaedia – defines world class as 'ranking amongst the foremost in the world; of an international standard of excellence; of the highest order'.

All these definitions support world-class performance as being based on best practices, benchmarking and excellent delivery. It will be seen from this chapter and also throughout this book that all of these factors are critical in order to determine a comparative and objective level of service quality.

The researcher's view

There are a number of robust industry models that define more closely what is meant by world class. The first of these examples described here relates to the characteristics of organizations measured by means of a research study carried out by three prestigious business schools of 310 service organizations operating in the UK and the USA and placing these in a classification system based on a service index (Voss *et al.* 1997). This service index rates the actual performance of the companies surveyed and also the degree to which best practices have been put in place, and is illustrated in Figure 1.1.

The service achievements of the 310 companies involved can be seen as a progression from bottom left to top right, displaying a strong correlation between the degree to which documented practices are used and actual

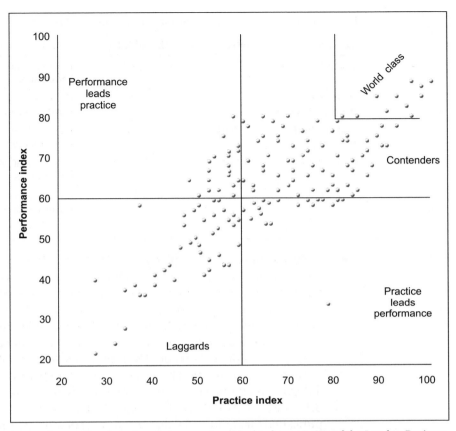

Source: International service study reproduced by kind permission of the London Business School

FIGURE 1.1 *Charting services against performance and practice indices*

delivery performance. Although this correlation is not universal, it is indicative of the first primary feature of a world-class organization – that when best practices are used consistently, they will lead to a high quality of service. The other two primary features of a world-class IT service organization, namely people and technology management, will be explained later in this chapter and also expanded in the rest of the book. The segmentation in Figure 1.1 shows how the companies were ranked in terms of their characteristics and Table 1.1 compares the UK and USA results.

TABLE 1.1   *Classifying services against performance and practice indices*

Category	United States	United Kingdom	Definitions – out of 100%
Laggards	11.1%	11.4%	Practice ≤ 60 Performance ≤ 60
Performance leads practice	17.1%	13.0%	Practice ≤ 60 Performance ≥ 60
Practice leads performance	2.0%	3.0%	Practice ≥ 60 Performance ≤ 60
Contenders	56.6%	67.2%	Practice > 60 but ≤ 80 Performance > 60 but ≤ 80
World class	13.2%	5.3%	Practice > 80 Performance > 80
Total	100%	100%	

- *Laggards* needs little explanation. They are those companies that neither deliver effective services nor display awareness of the importance of best practices in helping deliver world-class results. And yet the view of these companies is striking in that they display high motivation – 56 per cent of low-performing UK companies and 24 per cent of USA companies regarded themselves as being either completely or mostly competitive. This could be interpreted as a lack of understanding about the correlation between practice and performance, or even a degree of complacency about their ability to survive in a process-driven world. As details of the organizations in this survey were not published for commercial reasons, it is not possible to track how many of these companies are still in business.

- *Performance leads practice* is an interesting classification and one that contains a similar number of companies as the previous category. This is typified by a high-performance culture as measured by company output, but without the necessary supporting processes to provide stability or consistency. This is typical of an entrepreneurial enterprise or one that is relatively new and funding its way towards growth at the expense of process. As a stepping stone in service maturity, then, it could be regarded as a useful way of proving the business model and company viability before investing heavily in developing processes and management strategies. Companies falling into this classification will have a major weakness in that there is likely to be a high reliance on a few individuals, which, if they were to leave, could result in the company being without the necessary corporate knowledge – a collective memory – of how things are done.

- *Practice leads performance* is an area that has the least number of companies reported within it. This is a good thing because any company that has invested heavily in process management, enterprise resource planning (ERP) tools, reporting systems and management dashboards but does not show commensurate benefit from these is clearly in trouble. Again, it is not possible to track how many of these companies are still trading.

- *Contenders* is where the bulk of companies are placed and where it could be expected that the household names we rely on every day would have been ranked. This category supports the hypothesis that good performance derives from good processes, and it is interesting that there are more companies in this category in the UK than in the USA.

- *World class* is, of course, the category in which we are most interested. What this section shows is that organizations that continue their investment in effective processes continue to gain a benefit in terms of service performance. These are the companies with big reputations and will also be those that invest in their delivery, keeping their existing customers, winning new ones and probably scooping awards along the way. This is the category to which IT service delivery organizations should aspire and is one that is by no means impossible to achieve. The service practices that lead to this level of performance can be grouped into five different result areas – service process, leadership, people, performance management and results. As will be seen elsewhere in this book, this grouping is a common way of thinking about the actions that are needed to deliver effective results, and they apply as equally to IT service delivery as any other type of output.

The industry view

One of the leading organizations in the UK that recognizes high standards of service achievement is the *Management Today*/Unisys Service Excellence Awards Programme. This was established in 1995 with two primary aims:

- to recognize those organizations that excel at serving customers;
- to provide feedback and share good practices enabling entrants to improve their performance.

Although this awards programme is not aimed specifically at IT organizations, a number of IT service providers have entered and done well in the various categories – for example, Rackspace Managed Hosting was the overall winner in 2005 and Happy Computers won the top award in 2003, with both companies also scoring highly in at least one of the five component categories. This level of achievement, when service delivery is being compared across industry sectors by a consortium of judges drawn – among others – from *Management Today*, Cranfield School of Management and Unisys, a leading IT services company, represents outstanding performance and shows clearly that IT service must share the characteristics of all good service, regardless of sector. Not unlike the joint London Business School/USA Universities study referred to earlier in this section, the Service Excellence Awards Programme also assesses service performance in five categories, as shown Table 1.2.

TABLE 1.2 *Five areas of activity examined for the Service Excellence Awards*

Category	Description
Customer intelligence	This addresses how an organization builds an understanding of the needs and expectations of its customers and their perception of performance
Operational effectiveness	This examines the effectiveness of service delivery and how easy the organization is to do business with
Engaging people	This examines how well an organization inspires the hearts and minds of its people
Leadership and values	This addresses the direction and culture of an organization and how successfully values and leadership create a passion for customers
Organizational agility	This examines how well an organization anticipates and responds to the changing world

The awards take a broad perspective of service excellence, considering it to be everything an organization does to (profitably) win, satisfy and retain customers (citizens). The words in brackets reflect the emphasis given on two factors – first, that customers cannot be bought at any price, and second, that not all service providers are paid directly by their customers for the services they receive. This latter point is particularly important in the public sector, where egovernment targets are being progressively established and where public-sector organizations have a need to deliver world-class IT as an embedded part of their overall service – for instance, the National Health Service (NHS) has this as an objective for the National Programme for IT (NPfIT) – the largest IT renewal project in the world.

These awards are open to commercial, not-for-profit and charitable organizations of any size and, as already indicated, IT service companies can and do feature in the resultant awards. But is it really worth the cost, time and effort – and what is the motivation for entering in the first place? Addressing these in turn, the direct cost is not an issue – the entry fee is about £100 and so represents a notional contribution to the awards programme. Entering for an award involves completion of a structured questionnaire that probes the state of an organization's service capability against the five categories explained in Table 1.2 and should not take long for a relevant person to complete, therefore negating the concern about time. What then happens is that a shortlist is produced, typically involving the three highest-rated entries in each category; these companies receive a half-day visit from a team of assessors and may need to provide additional supporting evidence. So the cost is notional, the time to create an entry is probably no more than a day, and supporting the assessment visit is half a day – a low expense in terms of cost, time and effort. Of course, if your company is not shortlisted, then you may feel that even this level of investment is wasted, but the point is to look at the potential of winning rather than the downside of not being placed. If you never enter a competition, then you can never win one – and these awards are probably the cheapest form of benchmarking you will ever undertake, which is why they are being advocated here. Benchmarking is a vital activity for a company with an aspiration of being among the best, because otherwise it cannot be shown objectively what the status of your service really is.

The upside of gaining an award of this type is considerable. By entering, you get significant *personal* publicity – because service has a human face, it is not just a commodity product, as explained in the introduction to this book. Your *company* gets significant exposure in management circles through the medium of *Management Today* magazine, which is sent to all members of the Chartered Management Institute and is also available on general subscription, as well as significant coverage by Unisys, a leading IT services company. So it's all about the upside and not much downside – a very low-risk strategy.

The European view

Both the researcher's view and the industry view described above predominantly – but not exclusively – describe the state of service excellence in the UK. The study by the London Business School and the two USA universities compared the position in the UK with that in the USA, arguably one of the world's leading service cultures, whereas the MT/Unisys scheme accepts submissions from organizations that have been operating in the UK for more than a year.

Both of these perspectives are valid and offer valuable insights into what contributes to a world-class service organization. However, one approach that offers a view of excellent delivery that can be applied across national boundaries is the Excellence Model from the European Foundation for Quality Management (EFQM). The EFQM Excellence Model, which is represented in the UK by the British Quality Foundation, is used by some 20,000 companies across Europe as a way of defining and benchmarking the effectiveness and efficiency of their organization, both in terms of a reference against an absolute standard and in terms of identified peer groups. The researcher's view focused on the link between practice and performance in determining the route to world class, while the industry view looks at service performance in five different but related categories. The EFQM Excellence Model takes a wider perspective than both of these views by introducing nine criteria that allow the overall capability of an organization to be measured and reported, using a total of 32 sub-criteria. The EFQM Excellence Model also differs from the MT/Unisys awards scheme in that it actively supports self-assessment rather than relying solely on the views of external judges. Of course, if the Excellence Model is to be used competitively – and especially if there is a desire to achieve a Quality Award – then independent external assessment will be needed, although the majority of companies using the Excellence Model operate a self-assessment regime for very practical reasons.

An overview of the Excellence Model criteria is given in Figure 1.2. The model recognizes that achievement of excellent performance can be approached in a number of different ways, depending on company emphasis.

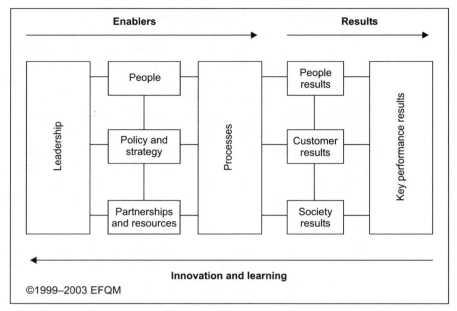

FIGURE 1.2   *EFQM Excellence Model, showing the nine principal criteria*

Like the previous two methods of assessing service quality, the EFQM Excellence Model is not written specifically for IT departments but it is as applicable to an IT service provider as to any other form of business operation. The model can be used company-wide or just within an operating division, making it very applicable to the management of an IT department, which is why it is introduced here. It is a viable means of determining and then measuring progress towards world class for a number of reasons, not least of which is that it is a numerically based model and therefore progress towards a defined standard of achievement can be readily tracked. This numerate approach can also appeal to the objective nature of many IT managers.

The Excellence Model is scored out of 1000 points, although the distribution of points throughout the nine criteria is not even. Figure 1.3 shows the distribution of weighting between criteria in the first half of the model, known as the enablers, with 50 per cent of the total score potential, and Figure 1.4 shows the weighting distribution across the second half of the model, known as the results. There is also a strong emphasis on linking achievements with the strategies needed to drive an organization, which is why an innovation and learning feedback loop is shown in the high-level model in Figure 1.2. This feedback provision is an important aspect of any system of control.

Figure 1.3 shows that processes is the highest-scoring criterion, followed by leadership. However, it is unlikely that good scores will be received in any of the criteria if a poor result is obtained in leadership, since by the nature of the model there is a cascade effect going from left to right and each criterion depends on its predecessor to some extent in order to set the context within which it can succeed. This also applies to the results area.

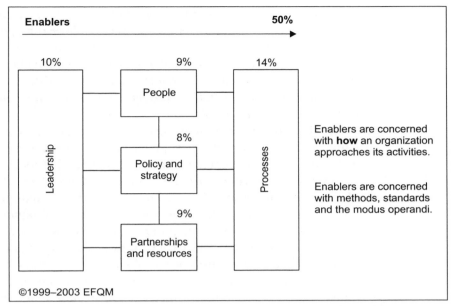

FIGURE 1.3   *EFQM Excellence Model, showing weighting of the enablers criteria*

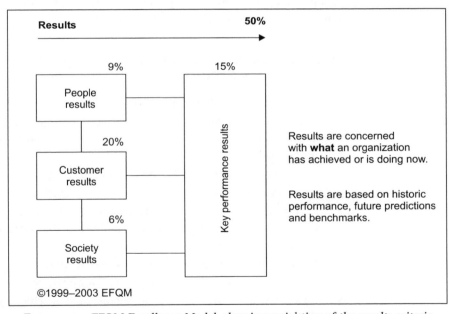

FIGURE 1.4   *EFQM Excellence Model, showing weighting of the results criteria*

Figure 1.4 shows that customer results is the highest-scoring criterion, followed by key performance results. However, it is unlikely that high scores will be attributed in the results section if a poor result is obtained in enablers, since by the nature of this model there is a cascade effect from left to right.

The ranking of the nine main criteria can clearly be seen as customer results contributing 20 per cent of the score, followed by people enablers and people results together making up 18 per cent of the total, and key performance results at 15 per cent. A strong implication of the main drivers of service quality is based therefore around the satisfaction of customer needs, by ensuring that staff are properly trained and motivated and have a focus on the expected results.

This situation can be summed up in the simple statement that 'first-choice employer leads to first-choice supplier'. This is an important point and we will return to this concept many times throughout this book.

Contained within the nine main criteria are 32 sub-criteria. In the interests of space, the full descriptions are not included here, although we will be returning to the implications of some of these in Chapter 4 on quality management. What is important to note, however, is the scoring attributed to these sub-criteria. The box below provides an explanation for three of them – people results, customer results and society results; the measures shown account for a degree of subjectivity by the introduction of perceptual, rather than purely quantitative, measures. Again, this underpins the author's primary assertion that service is not a commodity product, since the perceptions and aspirations of all the people involved in its delivery will make a difference to quality of service *as it is received*.

THE EFQM EXCELLENCE CRITERIA, SHOWING THE THREE PERCEPTUAL MEASURES

The three EFQM perceptual criteria are:

- *People results*: addresses what an organization is achieving in relation to its people, measuring results and the relevance of these measures in proportion:
  - perception measures (75 per cent of weighting);
  - performance indicators (25 per cent of weighting).
- *Customer results*: addresses what an organization is achieving in relation to external customers, measuring results and the relevance of these measures in proportion:
  - perception measures (75 per cent of weighting);
  - performance indicators (25 per cent of weighting).
- *Society results*: addresses what an organization is achieving in relation to society:
  - what is achieved locally, nationally and internationally;
  - the organization's approach to quality of life, environment and resources;
  - the relationship with bodies affecting or regulating the business.

  Society results measures results and the relevance of these measures in proportion:

- perception measures (25 per cent of weighting);
- performance indicators (75 per cent of weighting).

This box shows that staff and customer perceptual measures each contribute 75 per cent of the weighting in the criteria shown. As people and customer results are also the highest-scoring criteria, the model quite explicitly defines motivation, the treatment of people and the attitude with which service is delivered as very significant factors in the makeup of an excellent organization. When this is combined with those perceptual factors associated with society results, an area now more commonly known as corporate social responsibility (CSR), the significance of service excellence becomes even more pronounced. It is heavily influenced by the way in which service is delivered and not just how it is delivered – and this style matters to both customers and staff alike. The Excellence Model has been implemented widely across Europe and has inspired many significant improvement initiatives for factors such as staff and customer attitude surveys.

The Excellence Model is scored out of 1000, with the percentages attributed to each criterion being as already explained. But it is not necessary to achieve 1000 points, or 100 per cent, in order to be ranked as a world-class organization. The scoring regime recognizes the concept of progressive achievement where a company achieving 600 points can be classed as excellent, with exemplar companies, one of the true definitions of world class, recording 750 points. World class in EFQM terms therefore starts to be defined at 600 and not 1000 – and it is interesting to note that the average score achieved by companies submitting themselves for a European Quality Award – which is of course assessed externally – over a six-year period is 477. Figure 1.5 shows the distribution of assessment scores recorded by the British Quality Foundation between 1992 and 1998. Many of the organizations submitting themselves for awards here achieved recognition for excellence in one or more criteria – for example, in the 2005 Awards, Ricoh UK Products Ltd, an IT company, won the Achievement Award for demonstrating excellence in both corporate social responsibility and employee satisfaction and Siemens Medical Solutions, another high-technology company, scooped the Achievement Award for demonstrating excellence in customer satisfaction. These are demonstrably world-class results and we will look in more detail as to how the Excellence Model can be used as part of an overall IT quality management system in Chapter 4.

The professional's view

A number of membership organizations and professional bodies offer an awards process, and IT is no exception. Given that the theme of this book is world class and the scope is IT, only one scheme has been considered as an example in this section – the BCS IT Professional Awards. This scheme has been running for several years in association with *Computer Weekly* and was

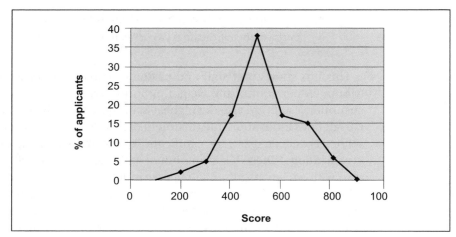

FIGURE 1.5   *Scoring profile for submissions to the European Quality Awards*

launched in its current form in 2003. The BCS regards the awards as having established themselves as a leading hallmark of success among IT practitioners, marking the contribution made by IT to economic prosperity, business efficiency and public services, and the awards are certainly supported very well by applicants, which shows that they have high perceived value.

The BCS awards process is a cross-industry event recognizing, promoting and acclaiming excellence, professionalism, innovation and the outstanding achievements which individuals and groups contribute to IT. Entries are made to one of five different categories – Business Achievement Awards (for excellence in IT management), Technology Awards (for technological innovation in a number of different categories), Individual Excellence Awards (for people making a particular personal contribution), Flagship Awards (for the most meritorious business achiever and the most innovative technological submission), and the President's Awards, which take a different theme each year. Recent presidential themes have included topics such as mobile computing, women in IT and information security.

The awards themselves are sponsored by major IT industry bodies, which provides credibility and industry exposure, while the judging is done by a mixture of BCS staff and senior BCS members on a voluntary basis. This mixture of input from a membership body and practising IT professionals maintains a healthy balance between impartiality and current best practice, ensuring that the judging criteria keep pace with industry developments and standards. Again, like the MT/Unisys Awards scheme, the BCS scheme is looking for best practices being established, not just being followed, but unlike the MT/Unisys Awards, this scheme is specifically for the IT industry.

The scheme has the same characteristics as the MT/Unisys process, sharing the same upside and minimal downside. Again, cost and effort can hardly be classed as an impediment to entering these awards – an entry fee of around £70 and the completion of a structured questionnaire, which ought to take a competent person less than a day to complete and – for those organizations selected for a site visit – about half a day to undergo an assessment. The view of this type of awards scheme is that they are an excellent way of benchmarking yourself and your capabilities against the industry, at low cost but with a big potential return. The typical cost of an IT benchmarking audit from one of the many companies specializing in this field is around £25,000 and therefore it is difficult to argue against the positive aspect of an industry award scheme of whatever type. More information on the BCS IT Professional Awards can be found at www.bcs.org.

THE SERVICE ACCESSION MODEL

We have looked in some depth at a number of definitions of world class and the processes and schemes by which attainment of world class can be demonstrated. With the exception of the BCS IT Professional Awards, all the other awards schemes are generic in that they can be applied as equally to business services as to IT, but they are also all applicable to IT services. As we have seen already, IT companies can do well in the MT/Unisys awards scheme and through external assessment against the EFQM Excellence Model, and the author commends them both; indeed, he has experience of the EFQM Excellence model being used to define service improvement initiatives for several organizations, both public-sector bodies and commercial companies. However, a characteristic that every scheme outlined in the previous section has in common is that awards can be achieved for a single activity and not for an holistic quality of service. This singular emphasis is meaningful in the context of the awards process to which it relates, but it does not of itself guarantee world-class quality in the specific context of IT service provision. As a result of this, the author developed an approach some years ago that was designed specifically for IT service delivery and takes into account the maturity stages in terms of both operational delivery and customer orientation. This is known as the Service Accession Model and is reproduced in Figure 1.6. It is called an accession model because IT departments can attain a particular *succession* of competency stages, each of which builds on what has gone before. The model can therefore be used both to define what is needed in order to reach world-class delivery standards and to chart progress towards its achievement.

This approach has been deployed in some of the largest companies in the UK, with the equivalent of 10 per cent of FTSE 100 companies having already been benchmarked against this model, and it is being used to define projects to demonstrate progressive attainment of higher status against it. The detailed characteristics of the Accession Model are also described in this chapter.

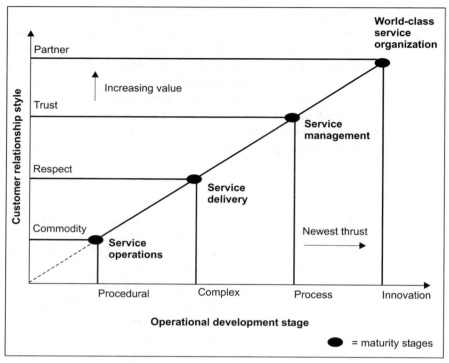

FIGURE 1.6 *Service Accession Model*

This model is different from any of those described so far, for a number of reasons. First, it is specific to IT service delivery and so is not a generic tool using generic language. Second, it requires equal emphasis to be given to the customer relationship style as it does to operational development, and this inhibits the model from being used solely to justify a singular initiative. Third, the characteristics of each of the four stages have been developed in terms of what they involve and standards of attainment defined, which allows achievement of this stage to be demonstrated properly.

There are four stages defined in this model, all of which exemplify the lifecycle maturity of an organization displaying the characteristics defined for each level. As explained already, each maturity level encompasses the one beneath it and so can be regarded as a cumulative, or progressive, status rather than something that is radically different from its predecessor. It is also possible for an IT department to operate at intermediate points in this model, which represents a continuous progression from bottom left to top right, based on how much of the maturity of the next stage is displayed.

Service operations

An IT department can be said to have the primary characteristics of a service operations team when the department is perceived by its users (or customers) as delivering a mainly commodity service and being controlled by strict operational procedures and standards. This is a positive situation in which to be, although of course it is not the status that many IT managers aspire to achieve. Operating at this level is exemplified by two major characteristics – the existence of (and adherence to) formal service level agreements (SLAs) and there being a rigid and well-documented change management regime. Although these characteristics are important, they do not engender a developmental relationship with the customer or demonstrate an ability to propose new services and ways of working to benefit that customer. Around 60 per cent of IT service delivery in the UK is believed to be operating at or around this level, which may seem to be a surprisingly high proportion. Many of the improvement initiatives in IT service delivery at this level are aimed at improving both the flexibility of operations and the perception of key customers, while keeping hold of the cost base.

Service delivery

Although the next stage is somewhat different from its predecessor, it is characterized by a similar set of values. The department still operates to defined SLAs and a prescriptive change management regime, but it now adds some value to the customer base by offering training to IT users. Training is almost always seen as a value-adding activity from an IT department and the reputation of service delivery is enhanced once this activity is brought into the relationship. Many training functions are housed outside IT – say, in personnel or individual line departments – and do not benefit from the synergy in terms of management oversight and value generation by having these departments as part of the IT competency pool.

This is not the same thing, however, as budget ownership. IT does not need to own the total training costs, since governance of such matters is often best left to profit centre managers, but IT does need to be able to decide on and manage training courses on behalf of its user base. The relationships between training companies and non-IT managers can give rise to poor commercial relationships and piecemeal procurement, which centralizing accountability within IT can avoid. It is surprising how few IT functions understand and deal with this issue – only around 40 per cent of UK service-delivery functions are believed to operate above the service operations level, with about 25 per cent of these being found at the service-delivery competency level. And yet the status of user relationship increases to include a degree of respect as IT is perceived to be operating at a higher complexity level by taking on board responsibility for training delivery, so it is clearly an important stage to reach.

Service management

This maturity stage introduces two additional attributes – supply chain management (SCM) and process competency. Supply chain management is not to be confused with procurement, although it certainly involves a significant element of that since it defines what and how service delivery needs to achieve in order to organize all the elements necessary for the delivery of an effective service. This can be likened to a prime contractor role, as in a builder who needs to schedule and manage plumbers and electricians and skills outside his or her direct control but under his or her overall operational umbrella. Service departments can be notoriously bad at subcontractor management, especially when these are through other IT functions such as applications development or information security, because of a perceived low management status. But getting a grip on the effective management of all the different components that make up a service is a key part of the competency requirements at this level, and SCM will be explored in greater depth in Chapters 4 and 7 of this book.

The second new attribute that distinguishes an IT department at this level is the emphasis on process management. In the world of service delivery, ITIL (IT Infrastructure Library, a collection of best-practice process definitions for service delivery created by and under the authority of the Office of Government Commerce, OGC) is the defacto published standard although it is not the only process framework in existence. Major IT companies, such as Accenture, IBM and Microsoft, have historically developed proprietary methodologies and frameworks although these are used in far fewer companies now than is ITIL, especially since the international ISO/IEC 20000 standard for service management published in late 2005 is based largely on ITIL process definitions, as was its earlier BS15000 predecessor. So developing and implementing formal process classifications for all the elements that make up an IT service is a key competency of a service management department and the structure, role and scope of ITIL is explored further in Chapter 4 of this book.

Only around a further 10 per cent or so of IT departments in the UK can claim to have reached this stage of service maturity, although those that have got a grip of supply chain and process development are generally trusted by their customer base because they are seen to be exerting control over their destiny.

World-class service organization

This stage is where the progressive IT services department should be aiming for. Building on the stages already outlined, the differences between achieving this level of performance and the previous one are characterized by one new attribute and a change of emphasis in respect of two others. The newest competency to be added is that of a sales and marketing capability, which service organizations are historically not structured to provide, but this should not be regarded as an additional function. The ability to represent what services can do, its prerequisites for doing work and a description of what value is added to the IT department as a consequence of the service strategies is a leadership task, not a cost overhead. Management of such activities will be embedded in the way the IT service management team (ITSM) thinks about its work and offers its services to the customer base, which enables the ITSM team to think exactly like a commercial organization would in the same circumstances. Not all world-class organizations are professional IT companies and not all professional IT companies are world-class service organizations – and the attribute of being able to properly represent your competencies to the customer is a large part of the difference.

The impact of service level management

Two other attributes, introduced in earlier stages, are subject to a change of emphasis on accession to this stage in the model. The first is that the emphasis on SLA management changes to become a focus on the impact of service delivery to the business unit or customer segment receiving it. This has been termed a business impact agreement (BIA) in order to differentiate it from the more usual mechanistic SLAs that cause so many problems. SLAs are frequently seen to be a bureaucratic overhead on the delivery of service, and something that the customer on the receiving end does not consult when formulating a complaint or when deciding how to deal with the IT provider. Equally, SLAs are often no longer regarded as a particularly valuable management tool by the IT department, because the linkage to the value of a service, especially when it has to be withdrawn, is rarely ever quantified and so IT staff do not know the actual cost of different levels of service. In contrast, a world-class service organization will be forming service relationships with its customer base in the knowledge of the economic value of that service in terms of how the customers use it to generate their own business value and can work with the customer to define the cost of ownership – including outage implications. In process terms this is not really different from how a conventional SLA is defined, but in reality it has a wholly different outcome as a result of the marketing approach used, as explained earlier. A BIA will govern relationships between supplier and customer at an altogether different level of management and lead to an enhanced level of management reporting – such as a discussion on future value-adding work as opposed to retrospective analysis of last month's downtime.

The impact of training

The second change of emphasis that characterizes a world-class organization above a good service management team is that concerned with training. Although the ability to train users in IT is a feature of both a good service delivery and a service management department, a world-class organization will take its training offering beyond just that of administration and delivery. What this involves for a delivery organization with internal users is that user competency targets are set and then a programme of training is put in place to ensure these targets are met. This may involve standard IT course offerings such as spreadsheets and presentations, but it will also require development of customized training in, say, business process design or workflow management. This is a very different style of operation because IT takes responsibility for the initial measurements to establish a baseline and then designs a series of training interventions to deliver a specified improvement against that baseline – with a 20 per cent competency improvement per annum being a reasonable target to start with. This is, of course, a challenge in that IT needs to be involved intimately with the departments in which these users are based and be able to understand the benefit of IT training on the productivity and effectiveness of the teams concerned. The other issue is also that of cost, since the analysis and development of customized training materials will inevitably lead to quite high cost levels, which will have to be justified. Here, IT owns the training process rather than the training budget and user departments will commit to any spend from their own operational expenditure – which is why they need to be convinced of the benefits. Quantifiable returns on investment in the range of 20–70 per cent or higher on IT training linked back to specific business outcomes such as higher productivity and lower staff numbers allow management decisions to be made that justify more effectively than anything else why IT training should be carried out. So the change of emphasis in respect of training is for IT to take responsibility for user IT competence, linked to tangible business benefits. This is especially important for organizations that experience a high turnover of staff, where productivity will inevitably decrease over time as trained staff leave, or where highly sophisticated ERP and management information system (MIS) applications are being operated by relatively junior and unskilled staff. There are many instances of effective initial training in such new applications, but rarely can case studies be found of where high levels of user/IT training engagement are sustained over more than the initial project rollout.

The situation where IT cannot control its user base, perhaps where customers do not belong to the same organization or where there is no effective business relationship, will prevent the level of dialogue and engagement described above. But this is not to say that effective IT skills cannot be delivered in such circumstances, as will be seen in Chapter 2 on defining the new role of service management. Based on the work done by the author in the past few years on service transformation, it is believed that no more than 5 per cent of IT departments in the UK are operating at a world-class level of delivery at present. But those that do operate at this level have found they are treated as a business partner by their parent organization rather than operating within a disposable service relationship.

THE CHARACTERISTICS OF WORLD-CLASS SERVICE DELIVERY

An IT services department that has been transformed through the four stages described by the Service Accession Model will exhibit six key attributes:

- *It will provide services to agreed standards.* This means that IT will define a service catalogue, agree this with its customers and then deliver an impeccable SLA performance against it. Although this is a basic bread-and-butter attribute, it is in fact very hard to deliver impeccable SLAs, especially when the service catalogue goes beyond basic service provision and when the SLA is now a BIA instead.

- *It will manage relationships with its customers.* This means that IT will proactively develop business-level dialogues that describe the current and future value of service delivery, as differentiated from systems delivery. This should show how IT services are allowing business targets to be met, what new services a business unit is likely to need in future and how these should be planned and delivered. It is most often found that new service requirements come out of the blue for service departments because they are based in the data centre or do not have management exposure at business level, in essence being regarded as a backroom team only to be called into view primarily to explain an outage.

- *It will plan and coordinate the delivery of change.* This means that effective change management regimes will be in place, encompassing both applications and infrastructure components. The scope of change management can be defined to include operational change control, release management, configuration management and licence management supporting conformance to both intellectual property (IP) rights and supplier commercial agreements. Change management is often thought of only in terms of basic operational control, whereas the correct interpretation of scope is that of managing the entire IT asset lifecycle.

- *It will develop and maintain supplier relationships.* Effective supply chain management, both internal and external to the organization, is a prerequisite for world-class status. The establishment and maintenance of supplier relationships, alternative means of supply as necessary, demand management, and good supplier relationships are clearly important to any organization that does not make and mend its own infrastructure. IT infrastructures today rely heavily on third-party service components, whether this be a managed network, a specialist company for desktop management or outsourced technical support. Seamlessly representing an extended supply chain to your customers is something at which a world-class team will excel.

- *It will provide technical and management frameworks.* Many organizations provide some form of infrastructure delivery change on the back of a new systems development. This can lead to a piecemeal approach to service management, as each technology and individual project team will form a different view of what management components may be needed. This is where an overall service framework should define for each and every project team what the standards need to be before their system can be accepted into service, and what technologies have been chosen to manage systems and infrastructure. Linked to the earlier points, the service management framework for everything from helpdesk to enterprise security administration should be defined in advance and published as a conformance document for internal and external suppliers alike to work to.

- *It will ensure customers derive best value from technology.* This is where training delivery and competency management will contribute to the overall world-class proposition. An organization that can help its customers to get the most out of the delivered technology, define an optimum level of productivity and then maintain their staff's ability to get the most from the total bundle of systems used by that customer is adding value, not just consuming cost. And, of course, helping customers to choose technologies with operability and manageability in mind will also define a better total cost of ownership (TCO) than would otherwise be the case.

In conclusion: what the Service Accession Model does is to show the four key life stages in the development of a world-class IT services proposition. The six primary characteristics of a world-class organization have been defined in terms of how they relate to operational competency, relationship style, strategic thinking and control of assets. Only around 5 per cent of IT departments in the UK are thought to be operating at this level, especially when taking into account the standards of attainment to which possession of such attributes must lead. There is little point in trying for good relationships with your suppliers, customers and business managers if the standards of service attainment are below that of your peer group, or are provided at a cost that exceeds what could sensibly be justified. There is a price associated with good quality in the same way that there is a cost associated with poor quality, and the price of good quality has to be shown to be less than the alternative. Chapter 8 describes the service attainment levels for a world-class service organization as achieved in practice and not just on paper.

SUMMARY

- Both world class and best practice are able to be defined.
- World class establishes best practice and is not fixed but will evolve over time as performance improves and management boundaries are tested.
- Benchmarking models and techniques are available to qualify world-class performance as well as any intermediate state.
- A world-class service delivery organization will manage customer results to at least the same standard as operational results.
- Competencies over and above traditional operational skills are needed to operate at world-class levels of service performance.

2 Service delivery

Chapter 1 described a progression towards world class by means of a Service Accession Model, which introduced a number of new delivery concepts. This chapter will expand on these concepts and explain how – and why – thinking about the role and value of service delivery should change for the better.

DEFINING THE NEW ROLE OF SERVICE MANAGEMENT

A world-class service organization will possess a number of characteristics that differentiate it from the departments that it supersedes. One of these characteristics is an emphasis on the use of formal process definitions as a means of introducing rigour and consistency, and ITIL can play the most significant part in this. Another new characteristic introduced in Chapter 1 is that of managing the end-to-end supply chain in order to effectively fulfil the role of prime service contractor, a role that most operational people intrinsically know should be done but often don't have the management scope or planning skills in order to do it properly – or are just too busy.

The third differentiator for a world-class team is that of being able to take on responsibility for defining and delivering a level of customer – or user – competency that is appropriate for the businesses that the team serves.

So how can this new role be adequately defined? The most effective way is to start with a close and critical analysis of how your service organization is operating today. This can be wholly internal or performed completely from outside, but to be most effective it is usual to develop a hybrid approach that takes staff members who know most about how the business runs today – current IT staff – and form these into a team with someone from outside who knows the bigger picture and can help address the perennial question of 'There's nothing wrong with what we do today – is there?' Unless you are already operating at the world-class level, there are changes that can be made to what you do today in order to add value to your organization. It doesn't matter whether you are an in-house function or an outsourced organization or even a shared-service operation – the same characteristics apply and will differentiate you from the wider marketplace.

Undertaking a baseline review is the first step in the process of discovering the potential for improvement. Figure 2.1 shows the relative positioning of service maturity in five major blue-chip corporations, some of which are run in-house and some as outsourced operations, in the UK in recent years. It is illuminating to see that few were operating at the peak of their potential, partly because the forward vision had not defined what that potential was and partly because it was difficult to see how to get there from where they were. All these companies started with a baseline review conducted by in-house staff operating in conjunction with an external facilitator, which led to a series of improvement opportunities being identified. It is of interest that all of these improvement projects, while attracting a cost to implement, showed a significant payback in many different ways – whether this was through improved productivity, actual cost reduction, improved customer relations or tangible improvements in service levels. Being open about the potential for change is the first prerequisite to being able to change – a key psychological principle.

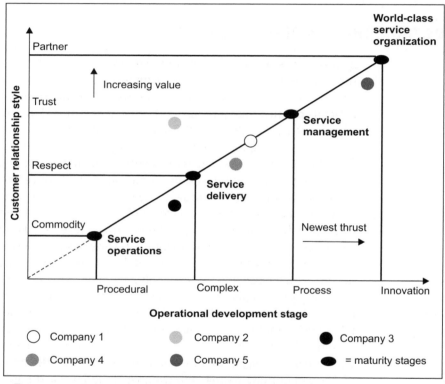

FIGURE 2.1 *Relative positioning of five major UK IT service delivery enterprises*

A baseline review, however undertaken, must include a number of key stakeholders in the process:

- the service operations management team;
- the wider IT function within which service operations sits;
- a representative section of the customer (user) community;
- the business management team – finance, marketing or personnel.

An introspective review sponsored purely from within operations is likely to lead to little, if any, sustainable proposals for change. This is because the appetite for IT change in the wider business will not be recognized and the enthusiasm of business colleagues for such change will not be taken into account. It is also the case that any projects arising from an introspective review will be given low priority in terms of financial evaluation and may lack the necessary political impetus to bring them to the attention of the authorizing body. And, most significantly – since an initial investment may be involved – the operations team may not own the capital budget.

Other factors that militate against a purely internal review are related to the three major new competencies that are required for world-class status. Process effectiveness, supply chain management and user competency improvements are skills that an in-house function could not reasonably be expected to possess when they are looking to baseline the operation – these are all future skills for which the competency will inevitably be found outside to start with. So what does initiating a service delivery review involve? This starts with the service team deciding that it wants to do work of higher value than it does today. Although this can be initiated by a new manager, it is also often done as a response to murmurings about whether the service ought to be outsourced. Outsourcing is often a reaction by a business to what it perceives as poor performance from its service team, either in terms of cost or delivery levels. It can also be triggered by a breakdown in relationships, which may arise from hard factors or perceived issues, which makes the politics of the situation even worse. Committing to review what is done today through a baseline audit is a way to demonstrate that the services team is open to discovery, and in terms of timing it is best to initiate this before one of the major industry outsourcing companies has made an appointment to see the managing director.

So the prerequisites for a baseline review can be stated as:

- a desire for change from the services team;
- an understanding from the business that more value can be delivered;
- current services are not under immediate threat of outsourcing;
- the ability to commit time and some money for external advice;
- a recognition that any changes made will lead to something positive.

The results of the baseline review should be an objective assessment of the current position, a set of proposals to move the service competency from where it is today and an overall indication of the time and cost to achieve. Engaging the business in terms of key stakeholders will have created an expectation that some change will happen and, if it is 'sold' correctly, will also have generated some enthusiasm for this change, which will involve their support. Timing is therefore critical – once the review is complete there is only a finite time before proposals for change based on the findings can be brought forward, otherwise the enthusiasm will have dissipated. Project plans coming forward up to two years after a review are irrelevant.

Once the review has been completed, you will have a definition of what your service department looks like today, what it ought to look like in the future and a set of proposals to take you on the journey. This is the start of your accession to world class.

COMPARING SERVICE MANAGEMENT AND OPERATIONS MANAGEMENT

We have already explored a number of factors that differentiate an operations department from the higher-order service delivery competencies. Apart from the three primary characteristics – process control, supply chain and user competency – highlighted above, one of the main enabling mechanisms for establishing management primacy over service delivery is the ability to reverse the typical IS workflow cascade. The norm since computer systems were first developed was that the business decided what it wanted to do and then the systems development function was given a mandate to develop an application to deliver it. There is nothing wrong with this sequence of events – except that most often the first time the operations team got to know about a new application going live was the request on a Friday to implement a complete new systems release ready for Monday morning. And this is the regime that typically applied to most IT functions throughout the golden age of systems development, ending in 2000 when it became obvious even to the layperson that the way in which computer systems were designed did not take account of basic logic flaws in relation to real-life situations. This also coincided with a huge upturn in the demand for online and real-time systems, many of which were accessible over the internet at any time of day, thus stressing the operational infrastructure in ways that a systems developer would not understand. So 2000, universally known as Y2K for exactly the same reasons that caused the potential systems crisis in the first place, did not only herald the point where computer programming shortcuts were a potential service hazard but also initiated a need for permanent change.

This is where the architectural inversion of the IT management hierarchy becomes a service management imperative. The best way of illustrating what is meant by an architectural inversion is by examination of Figure 2.2, which shows the situation that contrasts the typical IT department versus what is now needed to satisfy the demands of an 'always-on' infrastructure.

The left-hand cascade of Figure 2.2 shows what has historically been an appropriate way of taking a business concept from idea to realization. This has usually involved an accountable business manager deciding what needs to be done and then contracting a systems development team to realize that decision in terms of a product system of some type. The net result of this type of cascade is that the IT services team will end up inheriting whatever type of operations specification the business and development teams together are able to conceive, which may or may not reflect the capabilities of the available infrastructure or even any existing relationships with customers who receive services from that organization. The result is often a systems-specific operational specification and the cause of many concerns, which manifest themselves long after the project team has been disbanded. The people who inherit that situation, and who typically did not get involved in the service definition or even become aware of the impending release until very late in the cycle, are the people who get criticized for poor delivery.

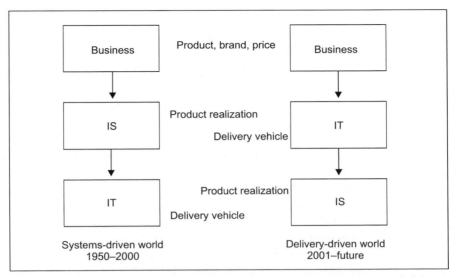

FIGURE 2.2   *Schematic of the architectural inversion relevant to current IT delivery*

This is clearly unfair, but more importantly it is also not representative of the contribution that a good services team can make to the resulting delivery.

The right-hand cascade in Figure 2.2 shows the way in which a world-class services organization can be expected to operate. Although there is still obviously a proper business relationship between systems development and the sponsoring business units, there is also now a service relationship that precedes it. This inversion should not necessarily be confused with a change of relationship management between business managers and systems development, which should continue almost as before. What the new service regime heralds is a parallel, symbiotic relationship between the sponsoring business and its service partner – note the term here: it is significant – in order to ensure the optimum method of achieving delivery. What this inversion means in practice is that the systems development function will already have been provided with a number of operational prerequisites that must be embedded in every new systems build. This specification will come from the service delivery department, which, as a consequence of its accession to world class, will have researched and formulated a service management approach that preordains things such as:

- the management agents that must sit on each and every new server or user PC;
- the application alerts that must be generated to the systems and network management consoles, and why;
- whether changes are required on the helpdesk to support the new service – including any changes to hours of support, or type of user;
- the planned service coverage – 24 × 7 or week days only;
- support and callout arrangements based on the agreed SLA;

- an assessment of how the new application will perform in a mixed service infrastructure – few new systems stand alone;
- the operations validation and assurance criteria.

The last points in this list are very significant. Modern service delivery infrastructures are like a motorway that allows a single vehicle to travel very quickly along it because there is no congestion. But, like a motorway, the delivery infrastructure has to carry mixed traffic and therefore the email service and the ecommerce application and, increasingly, voice traffic when represented as Voice over Internet Protocol (VoIP) all have to share the same network, access servers and structured cabling system. Performance issues will be highlighted in live use that would not be found in testing, and so a good simulation environment is vital for operations validation and assurance.

The box below shows the type of operational prerequisites that would be expected in a service framework specification issued to development. These statements can be expanded as much as necessary in terms of the specific requirements of each organization, and so what is shown here is generic.

OPERABILITY PRINCIPLES USED AS A CHECKLIST FOR NEW SYSTEMS DEVELOPMENT

- *The system must be operable.* Service delivery must be able to operate the system under normal day-to-day conditions within the cost constraints stated in the service level agreements and using the staffing profile agreed in the business case.
- *The system must be recoverable.* The system will be designed so that, within acceptable constraints, it is self-healing whenever possible from both a hardware and an application systems software perspective. Manual recovery, when necessitated, must be made quick and operator-friendly and, wherever possible, alert messages will be provided to operations staff.
- *The system must be maintainable.* The structure and documentation of the system must allow service delivery to make emergency and permanent fixes to those parts of the system that are handed over for support, with reasonable effort using an agreed staffing profile. The same principle will apply to code maintained by development areas. In this instance, there must also be an agreed level of service covering the incidents and the fixing of problems. Systems must not use hardware- or infrastructure-specific names e.g. server names, domain names, and file names.
- *The system must be capable of achieving agreed service levels.* Service levels must have been agreed formally with service delivery before presentation for operations validation. The service must be able to meet these reliably and within the level of authorized systems resource. Mechanisms must exist for monitoring of actual service against target service levels. Where contingency arrangements are required to sustain

adequate service during prolonged service outages, adequate procedures or facilities must have been designed and tested regularly. Systems will be developed such that they cost no more than the lifetime costs defined during the systems definition phase.

- *Operations must have been designed, built and tested.* The operations environment, including all required hardware, system software products, application software and documentation, must have been designed, built and tested. Any management needs for a new system must have been agreed with service delivery to ensure operational compatibility.

- *The system must be capable of being supported.* There must be a clear definition of how the system will be supported. Any necessary infrastructure (e.g. diagnosis tools, software distribution to remote sites, configuration control) must have been designed, built and tested. Procedures for support tasks must have been designed and agreed with service delivery, and any necessary training or familiarization provided before live operation.

- *The system must meet security, integrity and control, and automation requirements.* The requirements for security, integrity and controls must have been defined and agreed with the service stakeholders. These requirements must be met by the design and implementation. The system must be resilient to operator error as well as system failure, and automated wherever possible.

- *The system must be stable.* The system must be subject to a low failure rate and a low probability of functional or technical change in the period immediately following the commencement of live running. Any planned future release, e.g. corrections deferred at live running, must be scheduled at reasonable intervals following the introduction of a new service and any costs associated with this included in the business case.

- *The system must have a defined and recognizable upgrade path.* There must be a recognizable upgrade path for the entire platform in order to maintain currency. This upgrade path must be capable of being managed with the existing operational architecture. The system will be built so that predicted growth can be accommodated as business-as-usual activity.

Management of an overall service relationship with business units such that you are regarded as a partner and taking ownership of the quality dialogue with development teams is what differentiates service management from operations management. There has to be a reason to do this, of course, because otherwise the value of the effort put into making such a change will be lost on everyone, including your own team. So what is driving the need for change?

The drivers for change

The answer to that question has two components, both of which are quite different from each other. The first is that services are now offered around the clock and not only during normal business hours. One of the biggest social changes in recent years has undoubtedly been the development of a self-service culture. Today's consumers expect to order their shopping over the internet, manage their bank accounts from anywhere in the world and receive interactive messages on their mobiles. However, this can be satisfied only if the IT infrastructures supporting these services operate in a way that deliver such customer expectations.

Next time a customer logs on to your company systems, what do you expect them to do? With luck, you'll want them to order something from you, change their personal details or ask for some information – and given the nature of electronic systems, this expectation is now of a true 24 × 7 service. But as everyone in business has already experienced, many systems don't work all the time and the sign 'temporarily out of service' is highly frustrating. More than that, it can also be extremely expensive since customers are increasingly deciding on their bank, airtime provider or supermarket on the overall *service experience* rather than simply the product, brand or price charged. And this service experience is no longer the province of a customer services department since electronic access and fulfilment – self-service – have replaced the company person in a uniform so that customers now interact directly with the company's IT infrastructure. This is where it can start to get embarrassing: apart from those organizations that have been set up only to offer direct access, which are still in the minority, the rest of UK plc operates systems and infrastructure that were designed in the days when 98.5 per cent SLAs were the norm and Sundays were reserved for maintenance.

The social pattern of Sunday trading, 24-hour banking and the just-in-time characteristics of modern consumers dictates a quantum leap in the development of service infrastructure, based on an always-on philosophy. You don't have to be a telephone company or internet service provider to offer 100 per cent uptime and guaranteed responsiveness – you just need to be a bank or a retailer or a travel agent. Or any other company serving the public.

The public now form opinions of your company based on the ability of the IT infrastructure to satisfy their expectations. They will also let you know directly, publicly and embarrassingly if your IT lets them down – assuming they don't go to the newspapers first, that is. So how can UK plc better manage the service experience and satisfy the increasingly demanding expectations of today's IT-literate consumers? The answer is clearly that it can be done, and the paradox is that it is neither difficult nor expensive to achieve, although the solution does have a price. This price is a mindset change, which is difficult to quantify and certainly cannot be bought off the shelf. Starting on the journey to world class by asserting a service relationship with your customer base is imperative, even if it is difficult.

Figure 2.3 exemplifies the new demand for everything to be available online and in ever decreasing timescales, which dictates the service definition.

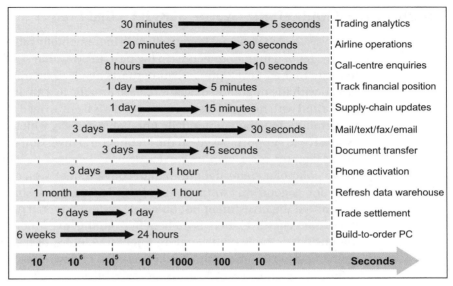

FIGURE 2.3   *Acceleration in business timescales*

The other factor that means IT service can no longer be relied upon as being delivered as a by-product of a new systems development is the issue of time and cost. In the early days of systems development, long build times using waterfall methodologies allowed some time in the schedule for consideration to be given to operations management, and the cost of a major project could bear the expenditure on some form of service management. However, as we have already seen, projects are not the best places for service delivery standards to be formulated and, in today's cost-conscious world, the sponsors of new applications certainly do not want to have a large bill associated with the delivery of something not connected directly to the original business idea. There is also no longer the time in a project schedule for the operations environment to be built, especially when the system is being developed offshore. The average time from specification to delivery of new systems has reduced by an order of magnitude in the past ten years, with many large companies now implementing the same number of projects in a month that they used to implement in a year. This is the result of incremental developments to existing core systems, such as building in more functionality and features, but it is also the result of the shorter planning horizons of companies that need to react to a change in the marketplace. Business planning cycles in the 1980s were typically five years long, whereas by the turn of the millennium few companies planned three years out and now the norm is to plan only up to one year – and sometimes less. This has implications for the way in which IT change is planned and delivered, both from the perspective of the forward view and also in the time it takes to respond.

DEFINING THE CHARACTERISTICS OF SERVICE COMPETENCY

When system changes are being delivered incrementally rather than through clearly defined major projects as in the past, the way that service teams need to relate to their development counterparts needs to be transformed. Being tasked with the migration of a new release into the live environment at short notice and with minimal testing frameworks is likely to lead to a poor-quality implementation and a potentially unreliable service, which will be, at best, expensive to support. Based on the architectural inversion described earlier in this chapter, it is clear that service delivery needs to be considered closer to the point of systems definition than conventional project methodologies allow for. A good way to think about this is that the business sponsor has committed the investment not on a new system but on a new service. Until the system goes live, there is no benefit from the investment put into it and the business case is predicated on forecast volumes of transactions over a defined period of time without consideration of downtime. Yet it is unusual to find any reference to SLAs in an approved business case and despite an SLA often being written for the resultant service, this is not accounted for in the project's authorized return on investment (ROI). The financial implications of this are explored in more detail in Chapter 5 but, as a practical example, think about a recent business case in your own organization and see whether it specifies how much service outage has been assumed in coming up with an ROI or discounted cash flows (DCF). Then ask your operations team whether it has built a delivery infrastructure to match the expectation of service that the new system will provide. The gap that will exist is worrying.

The changes needed in relationship style between the sponsoring business, the development function and the service team are profound. Figure 2.4 shows how the relationship between sponsor, development and service teams has historically been viewed and managed. This style of relationship supported the workflow exemplified by the left-hand side of the model in Figure 2.2 relating to a systems-driven world, which is now past.

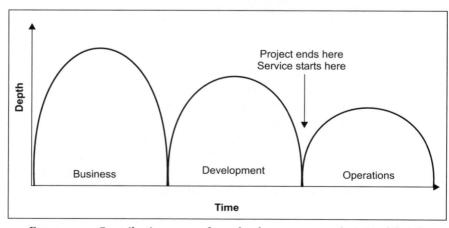

FIGURE 2.4   *Contribution curves for a development-centred project lifecycle*

This style is markedly different from what is needed to fulfil the architectural inversion as exemplified by the right-hand side of the model in Figure 2.2. For there to be a level of service that the delivery infrastructure can guarantee it is capable of providing, or for a new level of capability to be defined if it is not, the service delivery team needs to be engaged with each development from the earliest practical opportunity. This engagement role can be called a number of things – service assurance, service introduction or service validation; the name is less important than the fact that the service characteristics of every new development are defined in advance. What makes a real difference to the end result is that the service representative is able to work confidently with both the project team and the business sponsor to define what the operations staff will eventually manage; that representative also needs to have credibility within the services team. The characteristics of people able to operate in such a hybrid way are described in some depth in Chapter 3; Figure 2.5 shows what the working style results in. This involves engaging both the business sponsor and the development team in the service definition and then ensuring that the resultant build takes account of that throughout the project. Many organizations have run development and project delivery as a combined department, although this is becoming progressively less common as the linkage between standards of service and the speed of change shows that development is no longer best placed to own both aspects of delivery.

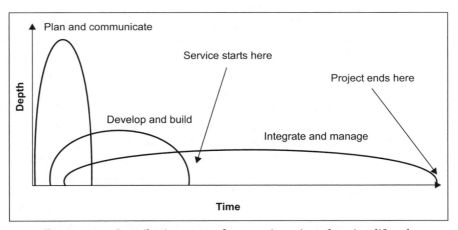

FIGURE 2.5 *Contribution curves for a service-oriented project lifecycle*

It can be seen from Figure 2.5 that the people responsible for service delivery should be engaged in the project formulation alongside the development team. The roles that each party plays throughout the course of a project are distinct and need not duplicate each other – developers will be accountable for satisfying any functional requirements and service delivery will be responsible for the non-functional requirements such as service levels, business continuity arrangements, access control and operational support. Early involvement in the project lifecycle will ensure that the new system enters live service with a known and predictable operational profile and a lifetime cost of ownership that has been included in the business case. Financial authority relating to the ongoing cost of operations is rarely considered by either business sponsors or their development partners because neither of them owns the budget for it and they may be reassigned to other initiatives when the system goes live. It is therefore important that the people who will inherit the new system for its planned life have a say in how the operational cost of ownership is optimized – after all, they are the people who have the most knowledge of how to do this. There may be no particular financial or operational implication arising from the new system, in which case the service delivery involvement in the project need not be more than a validation exercise. Most often, however, there will need to be a value-adding contribution from the operational inheritors in terms of service specification, type of support intervention required and also the financial implications of the new design. It may be that the new service requires a 30-minute response from operations support as opposed to a current four-hour response, or that the helpdesk traffic may increase as a result of adding a large number of new users. All these factors need to be assessed as part of the business analysis and systems design stages so the necessary costs can be included in the project authorization – or some mitigation of these costs if the resultant budget looks too high.

It is inevitable that any new system will have service expectations that will be more challenging than whatever has gone before. Figure 2.3 showed the change in business timescales resulting from using technology to drive the business processes and the issue of service immediacy places great demands on the infrastructure and the people that support it. A service-oriented project lifecycle as in Figure 2.5 will need to be underpinned by a service-level management rigour that reflects the degree of visibility that an online service attracts. When a system went down in the 1980s, it was likely that the overwhelming majority of customers would not be affected by it because it would probably have been a batch run. Service intervention was carried out by a team of dedicated operators, who restored the system and carried on processing, and no-one really knew how often this happened. This is obviously not the case in today's online, real-time service environment, where a failure will affect internal and external customers simultaneously and in a highly visible way. This means that the conventional SLA is being rapidly superseded, because of course there cannot be an SLA with the general public – the service either works or it doesn't and a call-centre agent telling people that the company has invested enough in the system design to support only a 362-day year is not viable – even if it might be true.

REDEFINING IT MANAGEMENT ROLES

The combined effects of service orientation in projects, a growing move to deliver all services on demand and a change to the established order of relationships with development and users lead to changes in IT management focus. The IT director, head of IS or chief information officer (CIO) – being taken here as synonymous with the same job – needs to spend less time on the bits and bytes than previously and more time setting and communicating the service vision. It is quite possible that the CIO will not have come through the IT ranks but will be from a different discipline – as long as he or she can define, communicate and deliver a service vision, then a technical background is not imperative. The CIO must be able to understand the terminology of service and rely on more traditional technological resources in order to flesh out the vision.

This effect can also be seen at other levels in the management hierarchy. Figure 2.6 describes the focus of a number of jobs in the IT service management chain for a world-class IT organization, and it can be seen that this is very different from the way in which such jobs have been viewed previously.

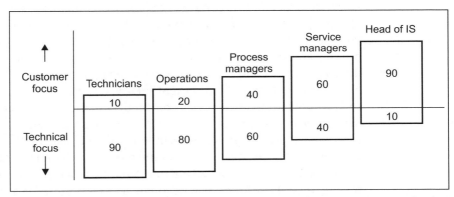

FIGURE 2.6 *Management time allocation for a world-class IT service organization*

Of particular note is that everyone in the service delivery chain needs to have some customer exposure. There are a number of reasons for this, which will be amplified in Chapters 3 and 6 and are also summarized here:

- The consequences of the actions of everyone in IT on the service being delivered have to be understood fully. The link between cause and effect for on-demand service delivery must be taken into account by everyone involved in the service chain, otherwise the chain will be broken. This linkage must be based on customer impact and implications, even if it has been caused by a member of staff who is unseen and unheard.
- Not all requests for service intervention can be fixed by an IT service desk and at some point a specialist will need to make a visit to the customer. These specialists need to know how to deal with a customer, even if their role in the company does not normally include regular

contact with customers – because that specialist represents the firm and will deliver what is known as an MOT – a moment of truth.

- Understanding your job in the context of the service that it delivers rather than on the mechanics of how to spend your day will give rise to a different way of doing that job. If every job in service delivery is aware of the contribution that it makes to the customer, then actions will be taken to ensure that the service chain remains intact and that it is treated as a priority. The best way of thinking about this is to treat the customer as if you were in their place – which you often are.

It can also be seen from Figure 2.6 that two IT management roles are shown between operations and the CIO or director. These are process managers and service managers and exemplify the level of thinking that underpins world-class delivery. Service managers are often thought of as part of the operations team, which they may well be, although that is often not the case. A service manager is the primary link between customer management and IT management and acts as a bilateral channel of communication between them, ensuring that customer needs are reflected properly in the IT service offering and also communicating IT services capabilities (and constraints) to the customer. A good service manager will appear to the customer that they are part of their team or represent their views while simultaneously being seen by the IT department as a control over inappropriate technology bias. Service managers can be employed by business units and sit with them or they can be part of the IT department, which is usually the case because the benefit to IT is greater than to the customer – and it can be difficult to get a customer to pay for such a role. Service managers will act as account managers for IT services, will negotiate and communicate service needs in both directions, and will act in the role of customer champion in project and infrastructure design meetings.

In contrast, process managers will own the quality and integrity of the management systems that underpin an IT service department. There should be one designated individual for each service process, of which there may be as many as 20 or 25 in a large IT department or as few as six in a small department. One individual can be responsible for more than one process but there cannot be more than one owner for each process – a single individual has to be accountable for the way that process works and how well it works. These roles do not need to be hierarchical in order to be effective. A process manager can sit at any level in the IT management structure and take instructions from people who are more senior but who do not themselves own a process, as long as the integrity of that process is not undermined. They will have undergone specialist training to run their process effectively and will regularly report how well it is doing in terms of quality measures that have been established by comparative or absolute benchmarking. They may also carry out other duties as well as owning their particular process and so need not be seen as a management overhead – the only process managers dedicated to the role but without some operational accountability are likely to be a performance manager and a quality systems manager, who respectively report on the achievements of IT and its compliance with established systems of control. Performance and quality management are both critical to the success of service delivery, as explained here and as will be seen from the detail provided in Chapters 3 and 4.

Moving from a conventional hierarchy to a process-oriented department involves focusing the efforts of IT staff into those roles that make most difference. The change from being a conventional operations department to a world-class service delivery one is characterized by a number of factors being emphasized at the expense of conventional management roles. This change in emphasis can best be seen in Figure 2.7, which highlights the new functions needing to be carried out and from where they can be sourced.

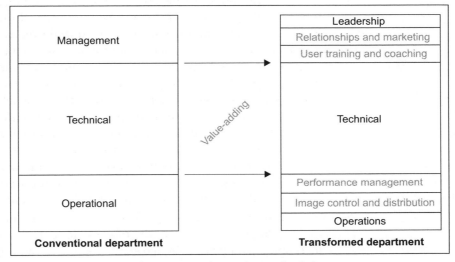

FIGURE 2.7 *Change in emphasis between conventional and transformed departments*

The new roles, shown on the right of Figure 2.7, are concerned with the effective management of service delivery rather than administration of day-to-day activities. Although process management is done throughout the department, Figure 2.7 highlights some functions, rather than processes, that need to be managed at an overall level:

- *Relationships and marketing*: relationships with the business, relationships with customers and relationships with staff are all vital to the effective delivery of services – remembering the assertion at the start of this book that service is not a product. Good service can be delivered only by motivated, trained, skilled and enthusiastic people, and the expression 'first-choice employer leads to first-choice supplier' has to be used again here. Equally, the way in which customers are treated and sold to – something that is rarely done well by services teams – will make a big difference to their perception of how good your service has been and therefore their level of willingness to continue to do business with you. Even if the customer is 'tied' to the organization, which may be the case for an in-house IT function delivering to an in-house business unit, it should not be assumed that the customer will always regard you as their preferred supplier. Many IT outsourcing initiatives start with an unhappy business unit starting to look around at external service offerings and coming up against professional sales and marketing people. Although it may not be appropriate to employ the level of sales skills that a third-party services provider will have, a certain level is most definitely necessary in order to reinforce and maintain a positive impression of the value and quality of your services.

- *User training and coaching*: user training and coaching is a vital function to undertake well. This can take a number of different forms, including formal training courses, customized events, floor-walking and telephone support as well as continuous user contact. Out of sight is often out of mind and the best way to retain a customer is to keep in touch with them by creating the opportunities for them to see, speak to or call you. The easiest people to see and the most helpful people in the company ought to be the IT training team because this is invariably where value is generated and, in the eyes of your customers, where the perception of value-adding activity in IT originates. People going back to their desks with more knowledge and confidence than they had before is a good way of demonstrating the value of effective service delivery, and the training manager should hold a senior IT position.

- *Performance management*: performance management is about controlling the quality and quantity of work done by the services team. Its scope encompasses service status reporting, although this is not of itself what the role exists to provide. Although SLAs will always be needed, the true worth of performance management is to set the standards for process effectiveness measures, monitor performance against these in conjunction with process owners and operate a balanced scorecard based on the attributes known to be of most interest to the customer base. Balanced scorecards are easy to construct but notoriously difficult to justify to an SLA-oriented mindset, which is why Chapter 3 will expand on this topic in some detail. One task that the performance manager has to carry out is a rolling benchmark of process and service measures against industry best practices and then adjusting the targets each year in light of these. Another performance management role, which is of especial importance to regulated industries, is to ensure compliance with the controls expected from a mature IT department, such as ISO or ITIL standards or the reporting requirements of the Sarbanes–Oxley Act. Quality-accredited companies, which are often third-party service organizations providing IS support as their main line of business, will almost always have

ISO 9000, ISO 17799 and, increasingly, ISO/IEC 20000 accreditation, and performance management in such organizations is seen as a key element of their overall service credibility.

- *Image control and distribution*: image control and distribution may seem rather obvious, but in fact they can be used as an important service-enhancing feature as well as something to enforce system controls. The way in which your services present themselves to your customers, the screens you use and the backgrounds you choose all make up an element of the overall service experience. User workstations can be manipulated from the service centre to display or reinforce the corporate message, publish new product details and provide links to important new services or corporate announcements. For example, you can use screen wallpaper to announce a new initiative or product launch to all staff when they first log on after the server profiles have been edited, meaning that no-one stays ignorant of the message or has to plough through endless pages on the internet, intranet or email, which is most often used for this purpose. Having control over what people see each day provides an indirect marketing channel between the service team and the customer and is another example of world-class service orientation that also maintains currency, as the messages can be refreshed as often as required. Having this capability means that other departments will work with IT to deliver their imperatives and thus enhance the service relationship in ways an SLA cannot.

It may appear that the size of the management team could get large as a consequence of the emphasis being given to these roles. The paradox is that management represents not a bigger overhead but a higher value, with the scale of the diagram in Figure 2.7 showing that conventional management and operational roles are transformed into the target roles at the expense of tradition.

One of the ways of achieving this economy in overheads is by extending the reporting hierarchy. Conventional IT family trees are typically made up on a 7:1 reporting ratio, where the number of subordinates in any function before a management job is created mitigates against large team sizes. With the move to a structure based on process orientation and functional authority, regardless of hierarchical position, the number of people that any one individual can manage increases to about 15, subject to personality and the overheads of whatever appraisal or performance management system is used. This is illustrated in Figure 2.8, which shows how process management takes over the conventional hierarchical management role in order to achieve this.

The change of emphasis in management roles in order to achieve world-class service orientation can be summarized as follows:

- Choose management roles on the basis of contribution, not hierarchy.
- Allocate priority to customer focus as required by the job role.

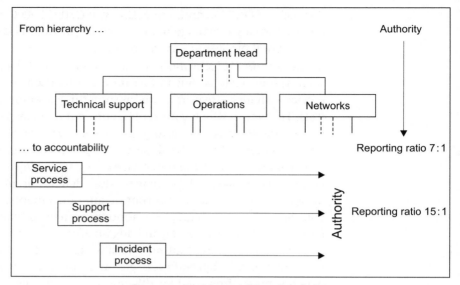

FIGURE 2.8 *Managing overheads between conventional and transformed departments*

- Appoint owners for each IT delivery process.
- Define and appoint people to the new roles of service manager, performance manager, training manager and relationships management.
- Restructure the department to avoid new roles becoming an overhead.

More detail about the characteristics of these roles is provided in Chapter 3.

SUMMARY

- Before undertaking a service transformation, carry out a baseline review to inform the project team about the most important objectives.
- Infrastructure standards and processes need to be established in advance of the systems projects that the organization will need to sponsor.
- Systems build times are getting shorter, and so infrastructure build, delivery and operation need to be highly responsive in order to keep pace.
- IT management roles are changing in favour of customer management.
- Process orientation will require fewer management jobs and allow the head count to be invested in new value-adding service propositions.

3 Developing the services value proposition

One of the big advantages of working in systems development is that it is comparatively easy to show what value you can add to a business. Whether this is by producing business cases showing a satisfactory return on investment (ROI), showing a project plan with a start, an end and all the milestones in between, or showing a positive post-implementation review is immaterial – the value of such work can still be demonstrated. This is not the same for a service delivery department because the management characteristics are different:

- Business cases for service projects are rarely produced.
- Project plans for ongoing services are obviously not needed.
- Post-implementation reports for ongoing services don't exist.

Because of this, service departments are often categorized as a necessary evil rather than as a value-adding team; worse, they may end up being seen as an *unnecessary* evil. This is disappointing because, as we have already seen in Chapter 2, the value of a new product is in the way it is serviced and delivered over its planned lifetime, not only during the construction, or project, phase. What is needed is that a positive view be generated of service delivery so that its intrinsic value can be communicated to, and appreciated by, all the necessary stakeholders. This necessitates use of a range of standard marketing practices and other management techniques, described in this chapter, to raise the awareness of the fact that service delivery operates 24 hours a day to deliver ongoing business value and is not simply a function to be regarded as out of sight, out of mind – or worse.

BENCHMARKING YOUR OPERATION

Taking these techniques in turn, a number of ways to add value can be identified. The first and most obvious is by benchmarking your service. As already discussed in Chapter 1, knowing where you stand against the industry and peer groups in your sector is vital operational knowledge and you should use benchmarking to check both the cost and the quality of your service against best-practice data. This will tell you what needs to change as well as what doesn't; assuming that you are prepared to modify your costs or service quality to align with the results of such benchmarks, then you will have something that can be publicized. Benchmark data are of little use on their own, and using such data to show that you are as good as, or better than, your peer group represents positive marketing. Benchmark data can and should be used internally, with a stated intention to repeat the exercise annually to ensure you are keeping pace with the industry. So what should be benchmarked? Service cost is an obvious metric because service delivery is price-sensitive and most outsourcing bids major on cost reduction as a means of demonstrating greater efficiency than an in-house team can show. There is no single answer to how much cheaper an outsourcer can provide an equivalent service compared with an in-house function and the author has observed a range of bids from +10 per cent to −60 per cent. The currently held view is that nothing less than a 30 per cent cost reduction is worth considering outsourcing a service based on cost alone, since value-added tax (VAT) and the hidden costs of service disruption are likely to negate any savings for the first few years. So benchmark service delivery cost annually on a metric that compares your delivery cost with the industry norm, recognizing that the comparison will be up to 12 months behind current rates, although whomever you use to help carry out the benchmark should be able to predict the trend in this instance. For an organization with large numbers of workstation-based customers, cost per seat – or cost per employee – is a reliable metric, whereas a company providing services to the wider public would most probably use cost per transaction instead. Some statistics for these benchmarks as at mid-2006 are included in Chapters 7 and 8 for reference.

Process benchmarking is another powerful way to assess where you stand against industry standards. Using either ITIL or ISO standards as a reference, you can go through each of the different process areas and find out how your practices stand up against the norms established for them. Figure 3.1 shows an example of this, for security management, by comparing the maturity of a real process against that defined by ISO 17799. The advantage of this approach is that it is repeatable, which means you can do it each year until you reach the required standard; it can be self-administered because the templates to do these assessments are readily available; and it also represents an absolute comparison to established best practices. There are 13 processes defined by the ITIL standards, which are explored in more detail in Chapter 4, conformance to which is a part of world-class delivery.

Other areas considered appropriate for benchmarking are the service standards themselves and a number of people metrics. Service standards are important because it is no use having a low-cost service that uses the best processes if the actual performance leaves something to be desired. Although SLAs will often define what the customer expects, these often do not take account of service attainment levels achieved in other organizations and they can rarely be relied on as a mechanism to retain customer satisfaction in the event of an outage within that SLA. Benchmarking the actual, or planned, service levels against your industry or peer group achievements will provide an important gap analysis that will provide an agenda for action as well as one of communication. For example, if a new automated teller machine (ATM) network has a planned availability of cash to customer, which is a true end-user measure rather than an IT-measured uptime metric, of 97 per cent, how do you know whether that is good enough? By comparing

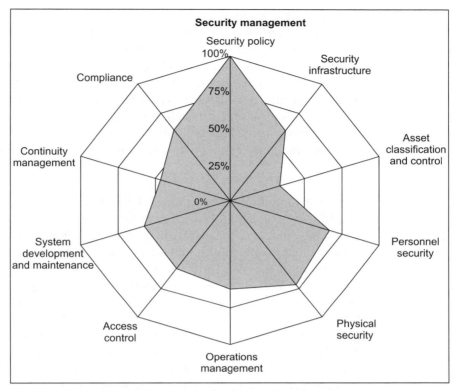

FIGURE 3.1 *Example of process benchmarking*

the same metric with that of other banks, you will be able to see whether your planned 97 per cent is good, bad or indifferent and then take action accordingly. If this level of attainment is higher than that of other banks, but is what your proposed class of service warrants, then you can make positive publicity from the figures. If the figure is worse than that of other banks, then you can use this information to help internally justify a different approach to cash replenishment or network planning. IT is often not the limiting factor in true end-to-end service delivery, but it can be the agent of change back into the wider organization. This can become known as a business impact agreement (BIA), as we will discover in Chapter 6.

Service attainment benchmarking is most often used in field engineering and technical support activities. Being able to assess your mobile engineering workforce attainment against current best practice will help inform whether your service standards are in line with the competition; similarly, it is essential to know what the industry service norms are when you are dealing with telephone support requests and order handling. Without such comparative data, the service offering is no more than a me-too activity, and world-class demands a lot more than just a mediocre offering. For instance, if you offer a home support service for PC maintenance, what level of engineer fix rates would you expect? What response would you plan to give through an IT helpdesk to sophisticated workstation users, and how do you know what your customers expect you to provide? Using your own staff and customers as informal benchmarks is always an informative process because they use more systems than you alone support and have experience of other IT providers, either by changes of job or because they are also customers of other companies. Asking them to help benchmark you is both relevant and good psychological practice to show that you are open to change and feedback, although most benchmarking exercises use outside specialists who have current figures based on their work with many other companies.

Benchmarking people

There are some important features of a service delivery organization that should also be benchmarked but rarely are – the people. Remembering that 'first-choice employer makes for a first-choice supplier' involves you in knowing what your people think about their work, what they have to do, how they do it, for whom they do it , and what motivates them to go the extra mile when necessary. Good service never results from a punitive approach to staffing levels and individual concerns, with leading organizations such as Scandinavian Airlines providing a good example of how staff empowerment leads to better service through having more motivated and committed people delivering at the point of consumption. Employee attitude surveys are an important part of any benchmarking exercise and will contribute towards the eventual attainment of world-class standards if you know what to aim for. Both EFQM and industry schemes such as the BCS Professional Development Accreditation standard rely on employee benchmarks and standards setting as means to accede to high levels of service performance.

Although most companies will be able to carry out employee satisfaction surveys on their own, expert help may be useful to set appropriate expectations and to ensure that the marking scheme aligns to best practice. A number of employee benchmarking processes are available, with one such example that can be used in the IT field being an integrated organizational framework devised by Steven Glowinkowski, an occupational psychologist that measures individual and team behaviours. The approach uses a series of diagnostic questionnaires to discover how people are predisposed to work and what organizational climate exists, which can be compared with a large database of norms and leads to the construction of action plans to modify the outcome in line with the service requirements. This need not be regarded purely as an attitude survey but also as an organizational diagnostic that discovers misalignments between people and processes and allows corrective action to be proposed. This type of tool is very powerful and is obviously an essential aid to world-class service accession, and it has been used to develop a role profile for CIOs in the UK as part of the joint IT industry working party involving the BCS, Intellect, e-Skills UK and the NCC as primary sponsors.

This shows a very high level of strategic buy-in to the concept of organizational benchmarking. More details about the Glowinkowski approach can be found at www.glowinkowski.com.

MARKETING YOUR ACHIEVEMENTS

An important marketing technique is to maintain the visibility of what you do. Service is invisible in that it is assumed to be there until something goes wrong to make it visible, but it is also transient in that once it has been achieved it is immediately forgotten. One way of getting more visibility of your achievements is to publicize them. The monthly SLA report is a standard way of doing this, although this is by far and away the worst type of service performance reporting mechanism possible, because it focuses on two things – retrospection and justification. Retrospection is bad because the reports look backwards at past performance, which is not necessarily indicative of what future service performance is going to be, and it also exposes IT to critique. It is very easy to criticise service providers for past failures since retrospective reporting plays to the negative side of human nature, allowing customers to focus on any SLA breaches or key performance indicator (KPI) shortfalls at your expense. In any event, it is very rare for service delivery operations to get an accolade for delivering to SLA, no matter how difficult that has been, because that is what customers pay for and expect you to do.

It is a paradox that appreciation of service delivery may come only in the wake of an adverse event. Dealing with something like a major virus incursion, an unforeseen business disaster or even recovery from a major systems failure is far more likely to give rise to a word of appreciation than doing your operational role day by day. Activity on problem avoidance, problem resolution and forward planning is far more of a management agenda than retrospective SLA reporting, which most customers don't read anyway unless they are looking for the justification to raise a complaint against you. It is this area of justification that also gives rise to problems with SLA reporting. What such reports produce are lengthy lists of meaningless statistics with attainment levels associated with them, rendering these also meaningless. Justifying an SLA delivery is seen by most businesspeople as defensive and, although this is sometimes necessary to support invoices for services provided, it should not be seen as the main rationale for service reporting. Producing a balanced scorecard of operational measures, of which the SLA is only one and certainly not top of the list, is far more meaningful and allows forward thinking rather than retrospective reporting which is of more use to both provider and recipient alike. Figure 3.2 is an example of a balanced scorecard for an IT services function, showing some of the measures that can be used. It is recommended that no more than 10 KPIs be selected as appropriate to your organization, and several of these should be forward looking in terms of what service delivery will be involved in next, such as new projects that are in the course of operations validation and any infrastructure development initiatives that are either proposed or under way. It should be noted that some KPIs will represent subjective data rather than purely quantitative measures.

Service Delivery Performance Measures – Calendar Year to Date

	Measure	Page No	12m to end 06	Latest	Curr Statu
Dashboard KPIs	Time to deliver an Order				
	- No. within 3 days	3	85.2%	0/0 [0%]	⟷
	- No. by date agreed		90.1%	123/138 [89.1%]	⬇
	- Average time to deliver		9.3 days	3.1 days	
	Incidents resolved at first point of contact [Tiers 1 and 2]	4	80.2%	75.7% [includes Sec Admin and Engineer calls]	⬇ 7
	Projects passing Service Delivery Criteria	12	96.4%	0/0 (100%)	⟷
	Staff commenting positively about communication	-	N/A	Employee Opinion Survey (GIS	◼
	S D costs per user per month	-	£1(P(9		
Service Control KPIs	Change Management	5			
	Service Level Attainm				

FIGURE 3.2   *Example of a balanced scorecard for service reporting*

Open all hours

Another key form of service marketing is to publicize major achievements throughout the year, or across years, in order to focus attention on the milestones passed rather than simply the number of SLAs attained. This can take a number of different forms, such as bulletin boards, inclusion of project implementations in the regular IT management reports and customer awareness sessions. Customer awareness sessions can be extremely positive, not least because there is usually a physical and logical separation between IT facilities and the people who use them, which means that few people are aware of what happens behind the scenes. Holding open days for staff and major customers in your data centre or network operations facility may not sound as if it will generate benefits, but experience across several industries suggests that it does. Several leading companies use their operational facilities as a showcase to demonstrate what it means to run a large and complex service environment in much the same way as the public likes to see the engine rooms of large ships and the flight decks of aircraft. Inviting people to spend time looking at what you have to worry about each day helps with subsequent conversations by allowing your customers to understand the processes that are involved in managing a complex service. It also allows the people engaged in front-line service delivery to meet their customers, which always leads to a better working relationship because it is easier to be abusive to someone you don't know than someone you do. Customers are invariably surprised to find how relatively few IT staff work on the helpdesk, since they have been accustomed to pictures of call centres occupying large warehouse-style buildings, which IT service provision does not normally do, although internet service providers (ISPs) and some other specialist organizations provide the exception to this rule. This works as well for external customers as it does for internal staff, although a strong caveat exists if an invitation is extended to members of the general public, since they may not generate the mutual benefit from open days as would the people for whom they are intended, who are, largely speaking, the decision makers, opinion formers and critical service users.

Arranging open days is one way of positive marketing where the customer comes to you. Of course, this can also work the other way round, since you should also be going out to see the customer and forward-thinking IT organizations operate a 'show-and-tell', or road-show approach to service marketing. Taking IT to customers is an alternative way of generating a dialogue about and awareness of the service proposition, which can be influenced positively by discussions around a presentation whiteboard. It is often a revelation to learn how little is known about IT constraints and budgets in a large organization, since relatively few user managers own an IT relationship and exercise prioritization mechanisms, but everyone in their department is a service customer of IT. The concept of enabled customers or power users managing an IT relationship is a satisfactory one, but it works much better if communication from IT to the host organization includes everyone. Mavis in accounts may be really frustrated that she can't get support for her new spreadsheet development, not knowing that a spreadsheet embargo has been imposed by her departmental manager who is happy to leave IT to tell Mavis that she can't have something that he hasn't told her is his decision in order to reduce development costs. Road shows play a big part in effective communication, without which the customer–supplier interaction is missing an important service dimension.

Make it visible in words

Another effective form of marketing is the service timeline approach, as shown in Figure 3.3. This involves nothing more complex than the production of a chart showing some key service highlights, few of which will otherwise remain in customer consciousness long after implementation. This issue of persistence is important in retaining customer awareness of the value of service delivery.

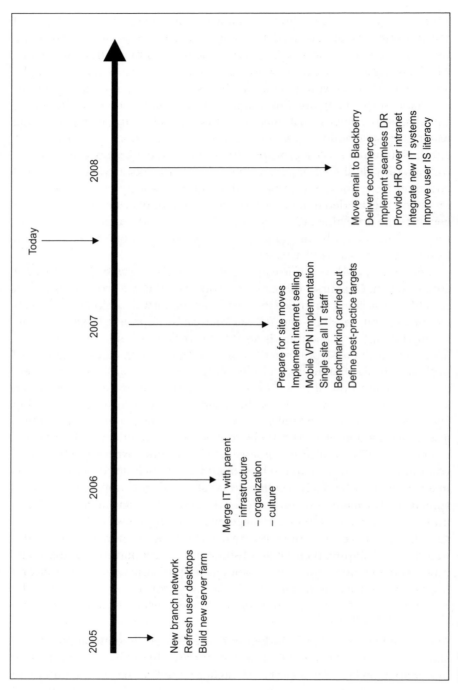

DR, disaster recovery; HR, human resources; VPN, virtual private network.

FIGURE 3.3 *Infrastructure timeline for raising service awareness*

When the role of the services department is being reviewed, little account is taken of what the team has needed to do historically. This is especially relevant when people are looking in detail at budgets and expenditure patterns, which may not compare favourably with their view of an operational cost base. This view may well have been provided by a competitor organization that has not included mandatory infrastructure development and a range of other must-haves in its pricing models, giving rise to a potential imbalance. So, one of the uses to which the service timeline can be put is to provide a context for budget consumption year on year, including a forward look as well as the obvious retrospective.

SKILLS, ROLES AND CULTURE

Service is not a product but the end result of a number of people cooperating to provide a customer experience. It may also involve a product as part of the overall delivery, but the essence of service is that it is an experience. This differentiates a service provider from a product provider in a number of ways, not least of which is in the organization that is needed to provide a seamless service when many different people are involved. The organization of a service delivery department differs from its development counterparts in a number of different ways, most notably:

- in the speed at which people are expected to react;
- in the way in which customers are dealt with, especially under stress;
- when things go wrong;
- when liaison with subcontractors or other IT departments is needed.

These factors do not have the same weighting in a project environment, and service delivery people need significant training and relationship skills in order to deliver world-class performance. An analogy between IT managers and theatre actors is appropriate at this point to try to demonstrate this. An actor rehearses for a long time in order to satisfy the role that he or she is expected to play, which the audience at any given performance is intended to appreciate. If this role is performed well once, then the audience is happy and so is the actor – this is a project analogy. However, if that actor has to perform the same parts to different audiences in different theatres on different weeks, regardless of whether the actor is being heckled, feeling unwell or having to get used to a different co-performer, the actor's skills need to be very different from those of a one-performance artist. The audience is different at each performance and one bad night affects everyone in the theatre: it is of little consolation to tell the audience that every other performance has been great and that it was unfortunate that this one wasn't – this is a service analogy. This difference is a major reason why the SLA is not used as often in leading service delivery organizations as in the past – a bad service experience is a bad service experience, regardless of whether service on other days or for other customers was to specification.

The skills needed to deliver world-class performance time after time are similar in both a top actor and a top services manager. They include leadership and motivation for other members of the cast (team), an ability to cope with changes to the script (specification), relationships with the production crew (operators), and interaction with the audience (customers). Yet it is often thought that services people, being largely behind the scenes – which is not true, because they are actually delivering the products of others – can get by with minimal management development. World-class companies expend significant amounts of time and money on training their service delivery people to achieve outstanding levels of performance – an initial level of 15 days on induction plus refresher training of between 2 and 5 days a year to enhance service techniques thereafter for every member of staff, in addition to any technical and product-specific courses. This is analogous to the rehearsal time needed by actors for their parts, which cannot be delivered without any preparation time, coaching or direction. Going live with only one short technical rehearsal before a major theatre production – or the operations validation process, in IT parlance – with no training in the system or performance prerequisites will lead to a failure to achieve the service standards that the customer expects.

Team work

Supporting your colleagues is an important hallmark of the services culture. Team work is essential in any discipline, of course, but the characteristics of that team ethos are quite different in service delivery and have to be evidenced for longer as well – service never stops, whereas projects do. Figure 3.4 shows one of the characteristics of team working relevant to a service culture where regardless of the job you do, a proportion of time has to be allocated to supporting your colleagues in an appropriate manner.

This allocation of time has not been determined arbitrarily but has arisen from operational experience. It has already been stated that service is a cooperative transaction between a supplier and a customer, and of course there are suppliers and customers both inside and outside IT. Equally, not every individual is in full control of the tasks that are necessary to deliver good service – few roles are genuinely autonomous, since they need input from other people. Although most individuals recognize when they need help *from* others, far fewer will recognize when help is needed *by* others, and it is important to build service teams with that recognition in mind. This section explores some of the techniques that can be used to build in beneficial dependency without ending up with a totally consensus-driven operation, which is not the desired end result – empowerment is vital, as will be seen in Chapter 6 when we explore the concept of the moment of truth.

A way to arrange teams within service delivery is therefore to build in a degree of role interdependency, supported by the enabling processes. This is illustrated in Figure 3.5, which shows a department consisting of six people, all of whom have defined roles, but they work as a coherent service team.

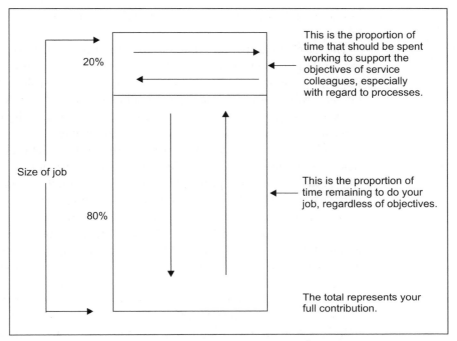

FIGURE 3.4   *The 80 : 20 rule for time allocation*

This concept requires each person, using the 80 : 20 principle, to proactively support their colleagues in the performance of their duties. This allows a specific depth of contribution to be made in the different functional disciplines, but it also supports a wide breadth to support overall service objectives. Customers need high service levels, aftercare, good ordering facilities and information about where their request has reached, which all compete for management time. By making the management team interdependent, none of these customer priorities is likely to get missed.

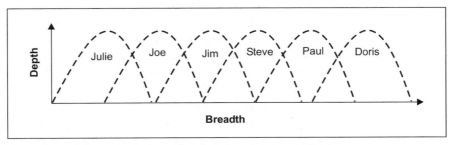

FIGURE 3.5   *Example of management contribution curves*

The contribution curve concept can be used both within a department and between departments in order to reinforce the service quality message. The wider the deployment, the more effective will be the result, and so this concept works best if it is organized at the process owner and senior management levels.

The job evaluation methodologies used to gauge contribution and relativities to other posts will recognize such interdependencies and attribute scores appropriately, although it is worth ensuring that each role is designed specifically to discharge prime responsibility for something. Not only will a consensus organization not achieve anything, but the role definitions will be too concerned with process at the expense of delivery.

Another valuable technique to focus the service delivery team on the desired outcome is the concept of a service-delivery value chain. An illustration of this is given in Figure 3.6, showing a traditional management view of service versus what the customer expects to happen – IT management being in possession of the customer's view of system performance.

It is very common for different IT departments to focus on the individual elements of the delivery chain without there being a coherent view of the end-to-end service (described objectively) or what the customer experiences (described subjectively). Customer opinions about IT are most often driven by a frustration that the service isn't working as it should or that when they speak to a helpdesk they aren't given an overall view. This is often because helpdesk staff are rewarded not on customer satisfaction measures but on call productivity, which, when coupled with the fact that they are rarely provided with service status information, means they can't provide an holistic answer to the customer. This is not the case within a world-class service organization, because there the service ethos means that customer satisfaction measures are defined and staff work to achieve those measures, together with a view being provided of the total service and the ability, if necessary, to mirror customer screens on the helpdesk in order to discover what the fault might be. These tools have existed for some time but do not always get used because their business rationale lies around customer fault resolution and not customer handling productivity. It takes a different vision to satisfy customers as a primary aim and to invest in service monitoring tools in order to provide the necessary end-to-end view, but the results of doing so can be quite remarkable. Companies with this vision and these tools can manage very high levels of uptime while still achieving high customer satisfaction rates based on few, but well-managed, outages. A good example of this is the UK post office, whose implementation of network banking to achieve chip-and-pin compliance not only was the largest example of its type in retail but also came in on time. It won the BCS IT Professional Awards in two categories in 2005, one for business achievement and another for project management. This is one evidence of world-class service orientation; another example features in the following case study.

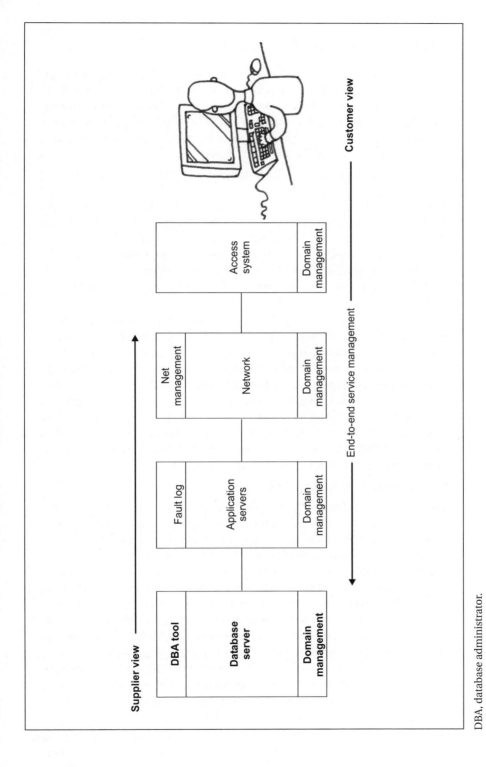

FIGURE 3.6 *Service-delivery value chain*

DBA, database administrator.

CASE STUDY – HILLARYS BLINDS

Hillarys Blinds Ltd is privately owned and is the UK's leading made-to-measure blinds specialist. It has a turnover of £85 million and commands 23 per cent of the market. Hillarys was formed in 1971 and has enjoyed consistent sales and profit growth throughout its history. In addition to window blinds, it also sells awnings and canopies. In 2006, it extended its product range still further to include interior shutters.

The Hillarys head office is in Nottingham. Hillarys has manufacturing operations in Nottingham and Washington, Tyne and Wear. It employs more than 900 people directly and has more than 850 self-employed full-time and part-time sales advisors nationwide who advise, measure, sell and install made-to-measure blinds. The majority of sales are directly to domestic customers in their homes as a result of an appointment with a sales advisor. The advisors work solely on commission. Each week, 8500 orders are processed and 25,000 blinds are sold, manufactured or fitted, from almost 800 fabrics and styles.

The Hillarys Group leverages its extensive manufacturing capability by supplying a comprehensive range of products and specialist fabrics into the trade and contract market. Consumers who are more DIY-focused can also buy online at www.web-blinds.com, the UK's leading made-to-measure blinds etailer. Hillarys has a traditionally structured ICT department with 15 staff. There is a systems development team comprising business analysts and programmers, and a technical support section comprising a helpdesk team and a systems administration team. The main business system is a customized SAP R/3 package running under Hewlett-Packard's version of UNIX and largely supported by Hillarys' own ICT staff.

THE SERVICE REQUIREMENT

Previously, sales advisors filled in paper order forms, writing down dimensions, fabric and other specifications and using paper price tables to cost an order. Customers can choose from almost 800 fabrics and styles, with literally millions of combinations of blind specifications possible. The paper forms, along with a deposit, were sent through the post to Hillarys; here, the deposit payment was processed in one office and then the order form was passed to another building for the blind specifications to be keyed in. Hillarys promises to fit the blinds at the customer's convenience, typically within 14–21 days. Three or four of those days could be taken up with just the posting and physical processing of the paper order forms. There was also a gap of three or four days before card payments were credited to Hillarys' bank account. In addition, around 20 per cent of orders were queried, for example because key blind specification elements were missing. Each query typically took five calls to get resolved, resulting in significant delay and inefficiency.

Advisors get their customer sales appointments from the Hillarys call centre. Prospective customers call the number printed on national and local media advertisements or leaflets to arrange a visit. The call centre manages the advisors' diaries and used to pass appointment details to the advisors by phone, fax, or email to those with internet access.

THE NEW SYSTEM

The ICT department and many advisors had for some time been keen to eliminate the paper handling and automate the process.

The outcome of the BCS-Award-winning Sales Advisor Mobilisation (SAM) project was a system that replicates the order process on a Vodafone hand-held device and sends the details to the SAP R/3 system as soon as an order is completed. The personal digital assistant (PDA) connects automatically to the central Hillarys system via the Vodafone GPRS network every three hours to collect details of new appointments and updates to product information.

The application also supports the sales cycle by leading the advisor through the process and ensures that all relevant data are entered and validated. The application then automatically prices the order, taking into account factors ranging from size and fabric to current promotional discounts. All this is done offline by the PDA, which means the system is not affected if there is a problem connecting to the Vodafone service.

Credit- and debit-card deposit payments are validated and processed online, so the cash is posted to Hillarys' bank account almost immediately. If there is no signal available, the card details are passed back to head office for manual processing the following day. There is little financial risk: Hillarys has all the customer details and can still check the credit-card payment before starting work on the order.

The system is secure too. All communications are encrypted using 128-bit Secure Sockets Layer (SSL) technology, and devices are authenticated using digital certificates.

Customer receipts are produced on a compact Brother thermal printer, which communicates with the PDA via a Bluetooth wireless link.

Once an order is complete, the PDA automatically transmits the order details to the central SAP system. Data are backed up automatically every night, including an image of the application. This means the PDA software and data can be restored automatically in the event of the battery failing or damage.

Skills and competencies

All of the service management techniques described so far can be achieved without recourse to published standards – they are not necessarily IT-specific although they have been developed to make IT service delivery credible. There are, however, skills and techniques that are specific to the IT world, with the most mature and comprehensive example of these being known as the Skills Framework for the Information Age (SFIA). SFIA is a high-level UK-government-backed competency framework describing all the roles within an IT function and the skills needed to fulfil them. The version of SFIA commercially available through the BCS – SFIA*plus*3 – enhances the 78 full skill definitions of the core framework by adding the training and development needs for each of those skills and the professional development activities, qualifications and career progression paths available. It is linked to the IS Examination Board (ISEB) practitioner as well as other academic qualifications and shows the relationship with chartered IT practitioner (CITP) and other classes of BCS membership. There are 78 skills defined by the SFIA framework and 263 tasks – which are the components of each skill – which cover the entire IT management lifecycle. There have been role definitions in the IT industry for some years, but SFIA*plus*3 is by far the most comprehensive and well-developed framework and has been written with significant input from practising IT professionals. It includes service provision as a specific competency; Table 3.1 shows the range and depth of service delivery skills. There are 17 skills defined exclusively for service provision, including some that may not have been regarded previously as being a services role, such as security administration.

TABLE 3.1   *Service provision category of SFIAplus3*

Category	Skill	Code	Level						
			1	2	3	4	5	6	7
Service provision									
Infrastructure	Configuration management	CFMG			3	4	5	6	
	Change management	CHMG			3	4	5	6	
	Capacity management	CPMG				4	5	6	
	System software	SYSP			3	4	5		
	Security administration	SCAD			3	4	5	6	
	Radio-frequency engineering	RFEN		2	3	4	5	6	
	Availability management	AVMT				4	5	6	
	Financial management for IT	FMIT				4	5	6	
Operation	Data protection	DPRO					5	6	
	Application support	ASUP		2	3	4	5		
	Management and operations	COPS	1	2	3	4	5	6	7
	Network control and operation	NTOP			3	4	5	6	
	Database administration	DBAD		2	3	4	5		
	Service level management	SLMO		2	3	4	5	6	7
User support	Network support	NTAS		2	3	4	5		
	Problem management	PBMG				4	5		
	Service desk and incident management	USUP	1	2	3	4	5		

Reproduced by kind permission of the SFIA Foundation

Table 3.1 shows the skills defined for service delivery and the levels of skill that exist for each subcategory within it on a scale of 1–7, with 7 representing the most senior level possible. This pattern can be seen across all of the 78 SFIA subcategories, and there are 16 level–7 skill definitions that offer a possible accession route to IT director, two of these being from service delivery, as can be seen here. However, it is not enough to simply progress along any single discipline in order to accede to the most senior jobs, but this does offer some insight into which types of job are seen as providing the essential professional grounding for a CIO or director. It seems inconceivable that a service provider with world-class ambitions would not wish to use the SFIA*plus*3 framework, or equivalent, to define the skills, training, development, career path and professional communities appropriate to their staff. Fortunately, SFIA*plus*3 is gaining wide adoption and is available in a number of manifestations – for example, as IT Job Describer or Skills Manager for use by employers, and as Career Builder for use by individuals. It is supported by a software tool to manage and automate the administration of schemes involving hundreds of staff and this tool can be used either under licence within an organization or at arm's length through a managed service provider. Further information about SFIA*plus*3 and the specific skills and career products that use it can be found at www.bcs.org.

Having a skill is often not enough unless it can be evidenced – just as in other professions, such as law and medicine. Service delivery skills, especially if developed through SFIA*plus*3, are capable of being evidenced and can be enhanced further by gaining specific certification. The IS Examinations Board (ISEB) in the UK and the Examination Institute for Information Science (EXIN) based in the Netherlands offer certification schemes based on formal training delivered by third-party providers and their own examinations. As the examinations are conducted separately from the training courses, there is a high level of consistency in the results, and both ISEB and EXIN are seeing high growth rates in the number of candidates coming forward for certification in the various service management disciplines – the foundation, practitioner and manager qualifications. An example of this growth rate is shown in Table 3.2 for the service management foundation certificate, the entry-level service delivery qualification, which is growing at double-digit percentages each year. This is indicative of how many people regard service delivery as a profession rather than just another job choice and should highlight the drive to achieve enhanced levels of service quality as a prerequisite to business survival.

There is a big opportunity for IT to demonstrate that it is a profession, in the same way as many people regard law or medicine, by using mechanisms such as SFIA and ISEB to describe the standards expected from each discipline. It is apparent from looking at the number of companies taking up the SFIA framework, and putting considerable numbers of their staff through structured training courses leading to certification in service management, that IT is increasingly being regarded as a profession and not an itinerant

TABLE 3.2   *Candidate numbers sitting the ISEB Foundation Certificate examination*

Foundation Certificate in IT Service Management

Financial year	Candidates	Pass	Fail	Pass (%)	Fail (%)
1995/1996	370	313	57	85	15
1996/1997	1030	679	351	66	34
1997/1998	983	695	288	71	29
1998/1999	1414	1243	171	88	12
1999/2000	2698	2286	412	85	15
2000/2001	3530	3273	257	93	7
2001/2002	7630	6521	1109	85	15
2002/2003	10 108	8986	1122	89	11
2003/2004	15 165	13 496	1669	89	11
2004/2005	23 090	20 009	3081	87	13
2005/2006	33 548	29 055	4493	87	13
(As at 30 April 2006)					

Figures provided courtesy of the ISEB

discipline. This is even more relevant when companies with operations outside the UK are considered as they are equally committing to defined levels of qualification and certification of both their people and their processes.

ORGANIZING FOR SERVICE

Professionalism is, however, of little use if the way in which the service is managed does not meet the needs of the service user. This is particularly concerning when the service that results from a high-profile project does not satisfy the needs of that service user, and this is often laid at the door of the service provider and not the project manager. It is true that a project manager and a service manager have different tasks and different skill sets, which often conflict, but the basic premise is that every IT project will result in a live IT service and therefore the voice of the services team must be heard as the project progresses through its lifecycle. This can be achieved in one of a number of different ways, the first being to understand the nature of the applications management lifecycle. This is defined by ITIL, as shown in Figure 3.7, as consisting of six stages, three of which are the domain of applications development and three in the domain of service management. There is a seventh stage as well, not described by ITIL but shown in Figure 3.7, as being a management role that ensures both the functional and non-functional requirements of a project are given the appropriate emphasis through the overall project lifecycle. This sequential staging model supports what was discussed in Chapter 2 but provides a different emphasis in that it gives not only a service input to the project cycle but also a project insight into the eventual service – that is particularly important when consideration is given to how service support should be organized.

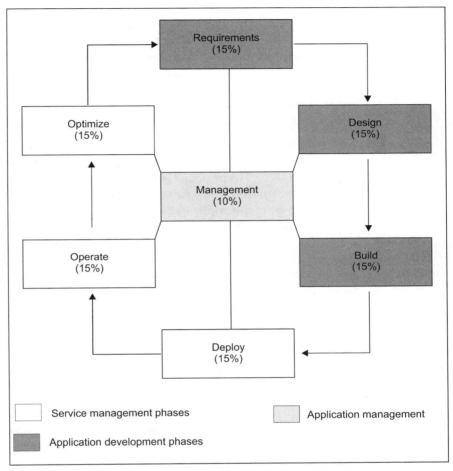

FIGURE 3.7   *Application management lifecycle*

Service delivery should be concerned not only with the three phases shown as Deploy, Operate and Optimize, although these are the phases that will take up most staff time. Equally, application developers should not be exclusively focused on the three phases shown as Requirements, Design and Build, although this will be their main area of focus. The main point being shown in Figure 3.7 is that the overall circle has to be maintained if a project is to enter service with an operational profile that is fit for purpose as defined by the eventual service user – any break in the circle represents a break in the service quality chain and will lead to a suboptimal result. The world-class team will look to avoid this at all costs because a project that delivers a disappointing user experience will invariably be one that is more expensive to run than it could have been and will also generate more management concerns, as exemplified by calls to the helpdesk, complaints and, possibly, loss of customers to organizations with better service propositions. This is an issue that effective service organizations can avoid by taking a number of actions:

- ensuring there is a level of governance sitting above the project;
- managing service development alongside the functional requirements;
- structuring support to provide the best possible level of service.

This section examines each of these areas in turn.

Service level governance

The way in which service governance is increasingly being viewed is that of adherence to formal standards such as ISO/IEC 20000 and Control Object-ives for Information Technology (CobiT), and these will be examined in more detail in Chapter 4. The principle behind any formal standard is more import-ant than the words used because of the focus on the end result. An alternative way of describing the applications management lifecycle is by means of a staged building-block approach, which means each contributor to a project needs to demonstrate added value rather than just being tolerated as a sig-natory to stage end progression, although that is important as well. Figure 3.8 shows the elements that different IT functions will be able to contribute to a new service; although they are all part of the overall IT delivery, each has to add value to what goes before it as well as representing what the customer should expect to see.

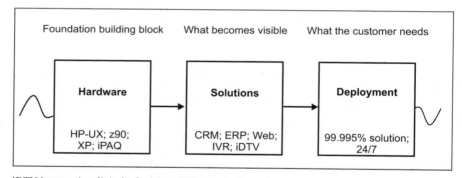

iDTV, interactive digital television; IVR, interactive voice response.

FIGURE 3.8   *Service value chain*

What this means in practice is that someone needs to be the champion of the eventual deployment. The question is whether this should be the service manager or the project manager – and why. There is more than one answer, depending on the management style of the organization, but increasingly it is becoming the prerogative of the service manager to arbitrate project deployment – or that of an independent third party such as IS Governance. This does not align well with many classical project methodologies, which is why they are changing to reflect the new IT order, as they must. A service that can never go down needs to have a systems architecture to enable that level of resilience; it is not an operational task alone to manage downtime. The emphasis of this section, however, is on the services team members to demonstrate their added value to new project development and not only to act as a brake on progress, which is easier to achieve. Designing for effective service mandates an understanding of both applications and operations and, as was seen earlier in this chapter, service level management is one of the few disciplines evidenced in the SFIA framework up to level 7. A role that can discharge the role of overall applications governance is the service level manager, or whatever title is given to the job, from inception.

Managing service development

How services add value to the project lifecycle is most often done by formalizing project stage signoff. This discipline is often used to effect stage progression in well-run projects, usually by the project or programme office; it is also used in the public sector, where an independent external body is used to oversee a process called gateway reviews. These reviews act as a formal audit that the project has indeed discharged what it should have done for that stage in its development, and work can proceed to the next stage only when a positive review has been given. This approach is also used by world-class companies to stage projects through to live operation by introducing a number of service checkpoints in the project lifecycle, which ensures a progressive development of the eventual service proposition. This approach means that service people need to attend project meetings, support their project colleagues in the development and definition of an effective operation, and ensure they add value and not simply build barriers to progress. The way this is best achieved is by aligning service checkpoints to the project development lifecycle under the control of the service introduction team, or an equivalent title, which exists to ensure an appropriate emphasis is given to operational issues at each stage. This approach is illustrated in Figure 3.9 applied to a typical project lifecycle.

Figure 3.9 shows that a project should be registered with change management right from inception. This is not standard practice in most organizations, although the rate of project development now mandates that it should be – contention for the few slots available for project implementation in a typical 24×7 organization means that the more notice that is provided, the better chance that project has of getting the relevant slot. This can best be illustrated by a piece of simple contention mathematics:

$C = N \times (N - 1)$

where C is the number of clashes and N is the number of projects

So, for an organization intending to implement 57 projects next month, there are $57 \times (57 - 1) = 3192$ possible ways in which they could interfere with one another. When this is loaded into the change management system, it can readily be seen why the performance of most organizations is not as good as it could be – few change managers are able to assess collateral project impact

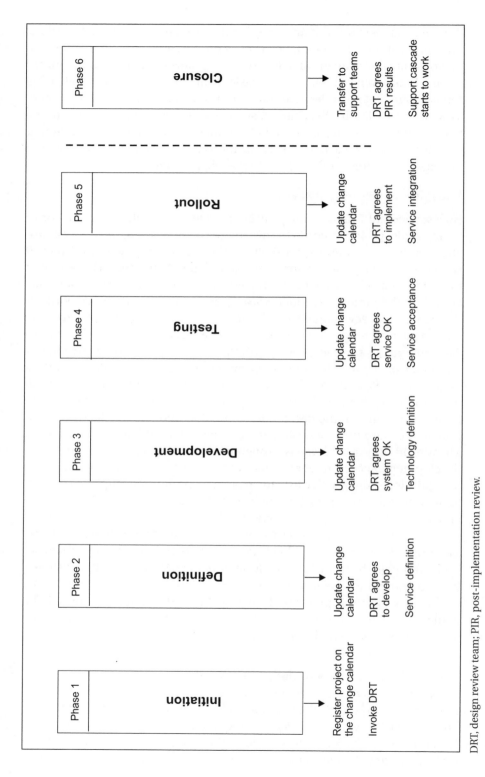

DRT, design review team; PIR, post-implementation review.

FIGURE 3.9   *Service checkpoints in the project lifecycle*

unless they understand, and have time to assess, the likely implementation issues.

Figure 3.9 also shows that a design review team (DRT) should be formed to act as a conscience for the service proposition, and this team should be tasked with ensuring that the service user is represented for their known, or anticipated, non-functional requirements such as tolerance to failure, service availability, response time, throughput, support and security needs. This DRT would normally be chaired by someone without a vested interest in either the project – thus mitigating concerns about project deadlines at any cost – or operations, who may have a reputation for negativity. DRT chairmanship may therefore be assigned to IS governance, service level management or an IT architect, depending on the nature of the organization.

By becoming involved in the development lifecycle in this way, the service delivery function can add value to the project by ensuring that the operational profile is as good as possible, not only for the new application but after consideration of everything else vying for infrastructure resources.

It is important to recognize that the project will remain under control of the nominated project or programme manager at all times and increasing service involvement is there to improve the end result, not take away responsibility from the project team. Service delivery will not be the only party with an interest in effective development, since the customer – or business – sponsor will also have a role to play and their needs have to be taken into account, as increasingly will the customers themselves. It has long been held that good practice in project development will include engaging a representative sample of end-users to help design, say, operational screen layout or the sequence of dialogues, because ultimately these people may be the ones dealing with a business customer using those screens. Take the example of a branch organization with a high cross-selling target imposed on its counter staff. These clerks need not only to deal with customer transaction requests but also to be able to access a disparate range of product, marketing and operational data in order to satisfy the request and meet any company requirements for cross-selling new products. This is difficult to achieve in the normal time that a customer would expect to wait for service unless the clerks themselves have had some input to the specification of how such a service would work in their environment. Several of the new skills definitions available through SFIA*plus*3 are concerned with the impact of human factors on development, such as systems ergonomics, non-functional needs analysis and usability evaluation, and so project managers can expect to find interest developing in these areas as well as the more conventional aspects of service such as uptime.

Best practice for developing any new business-to-consumer (B2C) offering increasingly supports the concept of customer involvement in service development. Although staff within a typical retail organization could expect to be involved in the development of a new service, there will be far less expectation of involvement from the customers of that organization. Yet leading consumer-oriented companies are taking the initiative in involving their customers in the design of new interactive services because it makes sense to do so from two perspectives – customer acceptance and cost of development. If a newly launched service can deliver faster customer take-up and acceptance, by involving a representative sample of current or likely customers recruited either directly or through a third-party marketing agency, then the business case for doing so will be strengthened. Customer panels are one way of doing this, but other techniques such as tracking the customer experience by the use of specialist website design tools, such as Gomez and Speed Trap, are gaining popularity because customer activity can be tracked and designs amended based on actual patterns of usage and preference. Similarly, by involving the likely audience in the design of a new service, project teams will be able to develop a look and feel that takes account of customer feedback and saves much time in developing functionality that few people will want to use. Companies that engage their customers in development prototyping have found an increase in customer loyalty and service take-up with a corresponding decrease in complaints because they are taking account of the actual needs of consumers rather than simply internal assumptions about them.

Support cascade

An issue that affects how IT development teams regard service delivery is based on organization – the traditional lines of demarcation between development, delivery and support. Increasing professionalism and the emphasis on qualifications such as the APM Certified Project Manager and ITIL Change Management Practitioner certificate are leading to a new generation of specialists who regard their role either as project manager or as service manager and who see it difficult to change roles without having to go through a new qualifications cycle. This is clearly not what is intended by the development of IT professionalism, and a retrenching back to organizational silos is certainly not what effective service development is about. There needs to be a progressive approach to personal and organizational competence based around the needs of the customer and, in terms of IT, this cannot be achieved by vertical silo specialization, although it is acknowledged that in IT, as in all professions, there will be some staff members who need specific rather than general competencies in order to do their jobs.

One way to achieve this is by ensuring that people who develop projects are involved in their eventual support and maintenance. A car engine designer who is not familiar with how mechanics have to repair the engine when it goes wrong will have a totally different approach to their work than someone who has a practical outlook. Car engines designed for low lifetime costs are designed in different ways from those designed purely for low production cost, and this approach can effectively be applied to IT developments. The way to approach this is through challenging the placement of application support teams within the development department – which is a common approach; however, the alignment of applications support to service delivery is an growing trend, driven by the realization that applications support is an operational task to satisfy demanding SLAs and the necessity for rapid intervention. It is not automatically the case, however, that aligning responsibilities in this way will work without careful planning; the two factors that need to be taken into account for a split of support from development to work well are *staffing levels* and *skills currency*. A working best practice guide for staff numbers needed for applications support is 6 : 1, as one person can support about six applications concurrently – assuming they have the right skills. People do not often move between delivery and support, and therefore formal handover mechanisms exist, often known as gateways, to transition responsibilities between different teams. It is clearly efficient to minimize the number of staff needed to support live applications, and one way to do this is to consider creating an applications support pool staffed by a mixture of core support staff and development staff from recently implemented projects based on a flush-through or rotational principle.

It is also unrealistic to expect that tier 2 application support – where tier 1 represents helpdesk application competency and tier 3 represents deep technical skills, either from a third-party supplier or an in-house specialist – will be able to support widely different systems without constant skills refreshing. This refreshing is also best achieved by the flush-through principle, where project staff move into support with a remit to skill core team members as well as support the application post-live, although this is not what happens outside leading service exemplar companies at present.

A key difference between ordinary companies and world-class companies is that some project staff become part of the core support team and members of the core support team cycle back into mainstream development, so keeping their skills current as well as gaining valuable business and operational insight. It is accepted that the personalities and orientation of support staff differ from those of development staff, and so not everyone will see such rotation as a preference, but this is where the business objective transcends personal agendas. It is often the case that support staff do not receive enough training to support applications based on service-oriented methodologies and this method ensures they do, in addition to gaining experience of new systems development technologies. Such a regime works best if associated with a strong resource-pool concept.

Figure 3.10 illustrates the flush-through concept for applications support.

Organizing the transition of project skills into service in this way will obviate the verticalism associated with project people only ever doing project work without taking account of the operational impact of their work. It will allow them to see what effect new systems methodologies have on the day-to-day operation of service delivery and, unlike a permanent job move, means they are likely to be able to go back to project work after an effective transition – unless they prefer permanent support work. This concept is sometimes referred to as a 'project warranty' period when the staff costs associated with

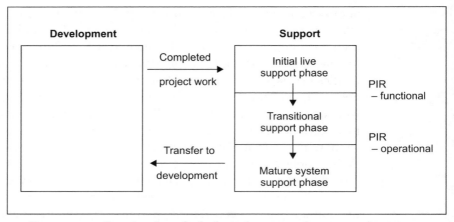

FIGURE 3.10   *Rotational, or flush-through, concept for new service support*

post-implementation support are provided through the project budget; this period needs to be managed carefully in order to avoid overspending against authorization, but it is a necessary part of an effective project to provide such transitional support to ensure a smooth-running and predictable service outcome.

SUMMARY

- Benchmarking should include costs, people, processes and performance metrics rather than being confined to technology or service level outputs.
- Market the service function so your customers understand what you do and what value you can add, as well as increasing management visibility.
- Teamwork is essential to the achievement of high service-performance levels and will mandate a different approach being taken to selection.
- Training, qualifications and accreditation are now well established for service delivery disciplines and should be used to improve and demonstrate professionalism.
- Management of applications support is increasingly being viewed as a service competency as it shares most of the management prerequisites.

4 Quality management

Quality is defined by the Oxford English Dictionary (OED) as being 'an attribute, property or special feature and which represents the degree or grade of excellence possessed'. It is also popularly regarded as being a mark of fitness for purpose – which is exactly what service is supposed to be about. Quality is often expressed solely in terms of procedural conformance, whereas it is actually about delivering what is needed by your customers all day, every day and until no longer needed.

This chapter explains how a focus on quality management helps service teams perform their jobs and describes the types of system available to prioritize their efforts. It has been deliberately positioned in the middle of the book because processes, and the systems that ensure process conformance, represent the pivot around which everything done in IT must revolve – they are central to the management of the department and must be treated as such.

DEFINING A QUALITY MANAGEMENT SYSTEM

The reaction of most people when presented with the word 'quality' is usually to conjure up an impression of something rather grandiose. The analogy of Rolls Royce and Mini cars often comes to mind, which is rather unfortunate because they are both quality vehicles – for the purposes for which they were designed, which are different. So how can quality be represented accurately in today's IT world, and what are the implications for service teams? In particular, how should a world-class team approach the issue of managing quality?

Ignoring this topic is a very bad option because if you've read this far, it should be clear that management of quality is all about planning and delivering good IT services. This, of course, is why the IT department exists. If this hasn't already happened, then you can reasonably expect your employing organizations to ask you to justify your management processes because of an approach from an outsourcing company, or a requirement from a customer for formal quality compliance, or – increasingly – because the regulator for your sector needs to see evidence of standards. Activity is growing in all three of these instances and at least something exists now that did not help those service departments in days gone by when BS5750 was the only game in town. ITIL, Six Sigma and a robust quality management system (QMS) such as the EFQM Excellence model and ISO/IEC 20000 will help any forward-looking service department to address any or all of the three above-mentioned management headaches. Although there will be work to achieve compliance, like any good medicine the taking of it is far less painful than the consequences of not taking it.

Management systems

Quality starts with the generation of a QMS, which at its basic level is a framework for the key records of what needs to be done, the processes to be used and what the outputs should be. This QMS should be the place where the targets, results and action plans of the IT organization are recorded and used as a constant reference for both suppliers *and their customers*. This last point is often ignored, which is a pity, since customers are involved intimately in the delivery of IT service and so should be included in the management cycle, as we have discussed already. The type of QMS used depends on the organization culture, the type of service offerings and what the relative positioning of the service needs to achieve. As the OED explains, quality represents the degree or grade of excellence possessed, and for some service organizations, such as outsourcers and group operations, which serve many different business units, there does need to be a quantifiable difference between what they achieve when compared with other organizations, with whom they may be competing.

The QMS is the place where these service aspirations are recorded and managed. There are many different types of QMS in use, ranging from the home-grown, through proprietary products that come with document management systems included within them, to robust industrial-strength frameworks. Examples of the latter type of QMS are ISO/IEC 20000, Six Sigma and the EFQM Excellence Model, which can be used separately or in combination, depending on the degree to which an organization wants to quantify and perhaps even needs to publicize its achievements. ISO/IEC 20000, Six Sigma and the EFQM Excellence model are covered in depth in this chapter, and the role of ISO 9000 is also outlined.

A good question at this point might be 'Which QMS is best for my organization?' The answer depends largely on how formal your organization is, what its service goals are and the degree to which these goals will be supported by the parent company. What can be said is that it is imperative for you to have a QMS, because otherwise you are working hard to achieve something that is neither formally specified nor aligned with the wider objectives of the service team – which have to be to provide services to a specification and at a cost agreed with your customer and to be able to prove that you have done so. How will you otherwise be able to demonstrate a value-adding contribution or to justify that invoice? This is the role of the QMS – to provide a quantified way of setting service targets and then defining the standards to which they will be delivered. This can best be characterized by the adage *if you don't know where you're going, any road will take you there*. Use the QMS as you would use a road map.

The role of ISO 9000

ISO 9000 has been around for a long time, even if the title may be unfamiliar. The most recent version is ISO 9000:2000 and may be more recognizable to some under its older BS5750 nomenclature. ISO is an international standards framework that can be used within only one country or between many different countries using the same terminology and standards everywhere – a must if you have international operations or aspirations in this direction. But even if you are based in the UK and provide services only to the UK, ISO 9000 is still relevant because it is one of the most easily recognized quality hallmarks. But does ISO 9000 help you to deliver better service? In isolation it can't do that, and some organizations have tried this approach and given up on it because the QMS was seen as peripheral to the service objective, not the driver of it. What ISO 9000 will do for you that is different from BS5750 is to allow process flowcharts to be held as managed objects in the QMS, perhaps using third-party tools such as Process Navigator and Quality Workbench Professional to map processes to any level of the operational hierarchy. Once the system is set up, it is easy to move between levels and to examine the detail of any process, since all the relationships are electronically managed – which means that any changes to one level will be reflected in all other views – as well as being in diagram format, which makes them easy to write, to understand and to amend. IS0 9000 is ideal for IT service functions, although it was not written specifically for that purpose; as we will see, however, the standard that is specific to IT can use all of the ISO 9000 attributes. ISO 9000 is most often used across IT functions, including development activity and where the specific auditing standards of TickIT apply. Organizations with TickIT accreditation include most of the big-name application management and outsourcing companies as well as many of the large IT concerns of leading blue-chip companies. These companies implemented ISO 9000 not because they had nothing better to do but because this was the best thing for them to do.

THE ROLES OF ISO/IEC 20000, SIX SIGMA AND THE EXCELLENCE MODEL

Although ISO 9000 has been mentioned in the preceding section and remains relevant for any organization considering external quality accreditation, this section focuses on other standards that have not been covered widely by other texts on service delivery. ISO 9000 has been around for a long time and is not specific to service delivery, but several other standards are.

ISO/IEC 20000

It will not have escaped the notice of most IT people that a new standard specifically covering service delivery has appeared. ISO/IEC 20000:2005 is the international standard for service management that was published on 15 December 2005, which makes it of especial interest to our community.

ISO/IEC 20000 replaced BS 15000 published on 27 September 2002 and is designed to promote the adoption of an integrated process approach to effectively deliver managed services to meet the requirements of both the IT business and its customers. This makes it applicable to every IT operation, not just outsourcing companies that rely on quality accreditation for their livelihoods. The standard specifies a number of closely related service management processes, as shown in Figure 4.1, and many of these will quickly be recognized as those already described through ITIL. So, it could be argued that ITIL has now come of age because an international standard exists to formalize its adoption – and this is a healthy sign of transition from adolescence to adulthood. ISO/IEC 20000 is in two parts, as such standards often are – part one covers the specification and part two is the code of practice.

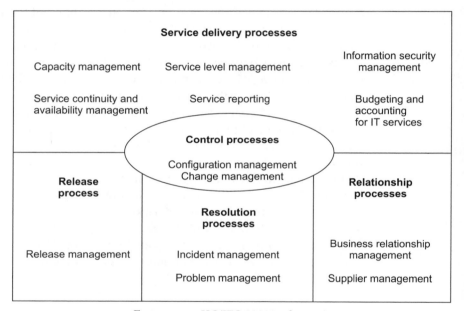

FIGURE 4.1   *ISO/IEC 20000 schematic*

But is process certification yet another overhead on already busy management teams? It certainly will be if adoption is seen as being in addition to how the service business is currently run, but, as many organizations already using EFQM or ISO 9000 have found, a robust QMS is the way in which quality is planned and how it is achieved. It is as indispensable as the word processor – and once implemented, it is as difficult to dispense with as asking someone to go back to using a typewriter.

ISO/IEC 20000 can be used in conjunction with both ISO 9000 and TickIT. As ISO 9000:2000 is process based, and ISO/IEC 20000 defines the services specification in process terms, then it is an incremental task to include ISO/IEC 20000 service element definitions within the ISO 9000 process structure. No wheels need to be reinvented in order to upgrade an existing ISO

9000 certification to include ISO/IEC 20000 compliance, and organizations with TickIT for development, but nothing specific covering service delivery, should think hard about extending the ISO scope by including ISO/IEC 20000 service processes, thus adding value to what may exist already in an organization.

However, it is important to note that three of the processes described in ISO/IEC 20000 are not addressed directly by ITIL. These three processes are information security management, business relationship management and supplier management, and so this chapter expands on these in order to provide a fuller explanation than will be gathered from the section on ITIL.

Information security management

The specification for ISO/IEC 20000 explains that ISO 17799, the international code of practice for information security management, provides guidance on how to address this specific process area. This aspect is important because adherence to ISO 17799 discharges the ISO/IEC 20000 objectives and controls for security management without further work and so the two standards can be regarded as joint contributors to an effective service delivery regime. It is possible to attain certification in one area without the other, but the amount of work likely to achieve ISO/IEC 20000 on its own will be underestimated without consideration of the essential components drawn from ISO 17799, which is described specifically in Chapter 7.

Business relationship management

This is described by ITIL and is most often taken to refer to service level management and, more specifically, to the SLA. However, the objective of such a relationship management system is much wider than the definition of an SLA, and ISO/IEC 20000 explains that the objective is to establish and maintain a good relationship based on understanding the customer and their business needs. An SLA is part of this, as is the nomination of individuals in the service delivery organization responsible for managing customer satisfaction and the overall relationship process. In some organizations, the only nominated individual is the CIO, by default, when this aspect is overlooked, whereas in most organizations there will be some form of customer service function, often the helpdesk but increasingly a service manager for each defined customer.

ISO/IEC 20000 specifies that a process should exist to obtain and act upon feedback from regular customer satisfaction measures and that actions should be identified during this process for inclusion in a plan to improve the service – which is not only best practice but obvious good practice. Despite this, properly designed customer satisfaction measures are hard to find, except in the top-performing companies, simply because service is regarded as being open-ended rather than as part of a closed-loop system with effective feedback mechanisms, which modern standards have been designed to provide. Of course, feedback is a two-way process, and the objective for the relationship manager is to ensure not only that the service provider is aware of how their service has been received but that the service receiver provides adequate information to the provider in order to allow any new or changed business needs to be assessed properly and satisfied professionally. This relationship role can be discharged either from within the business unit or from either the IT department overall or the service department alone, depending on the relative weighting of development to service criticality. Irrespective of which team provides the relationship role, however, the person responsible for discharging it should be accountable to both the business and IT jointly in order to avoid the accusation of 'going native' in one sense or to merely become the purveyor of service outage news, which is a part of but not the whole rationale for the job.

Supplier management

The objective of a services department is clearly one of service integration, since the department is providing something based on a mix of proprietary components such as hardware and operating systems, third-party services, custom-designed systems, packaged applications and communications networks. Service delivery is rarely the place where the management of all these elements is drawn together, whereas ISO/IEC 20000 specifies that it needs to be. The standard calls for the service provider to have documented supplier management processes and to name a contract manager responsible for each supplier, which will be documented and agreed by all concerned. More importantly, the interfaces between processes used by each party need to be documented and agreed to ensure seamless integration of the different components, and this is covered in more detail in Chapter 7.

So, these three process areas described by ISO/IEC 20000 are not addressed solely by ITIL, which means that techniques drawn from elsewhere will also be needed in order to address the full scope of the standard and support accreditation.

Six Sigma

Six Sigma is not a generic QMS in the same way as ISO 9000, ISO/IEC 20000 and the Excellence Model are, but it can be used either independently or in conjunction with them. In its most basic form, Six Sigma defines quality as a representation of the number of defects allowed in each 1 million occurrences of an event, whether that be in service or manufacturing disciplines. It originated in the manufacturing industry in the 1980s and is now used widely across all industry sectors, since quality of service is rapidly being regarded as important as quality in manufacturing, especially as manufacturing increasingly moves outside the UK. Sigma is a Greek word used by statisticians to represent the standard deviation of a particular population of data. The standard deviation of a set of data shows how much variability there is within a group of items in a chosen sample; the more variation there is, the larger the standard deviation becomes. Six Sigma therefore has the goal of focusing on the achievement of very small standard deviations from the stated goal so that almost everything meets the design target. A single sigma, or standard deviation, represents 691,462 defects per 1 million occurrences; the progressive representation of higher levels of attainment is shown in Table 4.1.

TABLE 4.1   *Representation of Six Sigma defect rates*

Sigma	Defects per 1 million	Quality representation (%)
1	691,462	30.85
2	308,537	69.15
3	66,807	93.32
4	6210	99.38
5	233	99.98
6	3.4	99.9997

If these statistics are applied to an IT department, then it can quickly be seen that typical development and service delivery departments, using different measures but represented in the same way statistically, will be around sigma level 4. Some service departments could claim to be at sigma level 5 if their delivery achieves stated goals as often as shown here, but this is unusual – unless the goals are so understated that they are easy to achieve. Modern customer demands usually mean that the targets have to be very high, and the higher they are, the less likely it is that they will be reached consistently, which is what high sigma levels actually represent. Clearly, Six Sigma is the goal that world-class companies should strive to attain, and in practice there is significant benefit that can be gained from service delivery approaching this level, as seen in the case study in this chapter.

What a high-performing organization achieves by adopting an approach like Six Sigma is a significant reduction in service variability, which is important in the eyes of a customer. If a service works in a particular way today, then it should work in the same way tomorrow and not be characterized by achieving a specified average standard, regardless of fluctuations and failures. One way of doing this is by applying such techniques as the Six Sigma method define, measure, analyse, improve and control (DMAIC), to help focus attention on what matters to the customer. A number of other techniques that align to DMAIC are critical to quality (CTQ) measures, which are service elements defined by the customer as being of particular importance; voice of the customer (VOC), which captures CTQs in an understandable way; and failure modes and effect analysis (FMEA), which examines the potential for failure and the effect a failure may have on a system or process. If these techniques are used properly, then the result can be dramatic, as illustrated in the following real-life example.

CASE STUDY BASED ON SIX SIGMA

This example is taken from work done for a major international retailer of travel tickets. The company sold tickets for travel through an online ordering system based on a browser interface on their website and then through a number of internal systems linking to a complex revenue-management algorithm that decided what to charge for tickets depending on time of day, volume of tickets sold, number of seats available and other pricing strategies such as special promotions. As the system was available to any customer in the world, it had a true 24×7 availability requirement, but the business case for investing in a higher level of availability than was being achieved was hard for IT to justify. Interviews were arranged with the business owners of this service to discover the value of each sale, the opportunity loss of each failed sale and the likely volume of sales each year. This VOC exercise revealed a number of important characteristics:

- The loss of ticket sales was irreversible – customers simply went elsewhere if the online booking service was unavailable.

- Service costs were predicated on a project budget and not on service value.

- The order-taking system generated £250/minute sales revenue.

Based on this, the following analysis was carried out:

Uptime		Service downtime
Actual SLA attainment:	99.5%	43¾ hours/year
Best-practice level:	99.995%	26¼ minutes/year

As every order missed is deemed to be irretrievable, the loss of income was:

Service downtime		Loss of income
Actual SLA attainment:	43¾ hours/year	£650,430
Best-practice level:	26¼ minutes/year	£ 6570

The margin made on each ticket was 20 per cent, and so the actual loss to bottom-line profitability from a loss of income of around £650,000 a year was £128,772.

This level of benefit justified a re-engineering exercise to increase the overall availability from 99.5 per cent to 99.995 per cent, nearly sigma level 6, which was the level agreed as being achievable, with payback within one year. This resulted in a better service, a happier customer and an IT department that needed to do less firefighting and that now knew the business value of its service.

This simple example shows what holistic analysis can achieve in terms of service value, but that is not all that Six Sigma can be used for. The technique can be used with equal effect to assess and control staff and customer satisfaction levels, the level of process malfunction within IT, and even how effectively team leaders act in terms of setting and achieving targets. It is a technique that can be used anywhere, like ISO 9000, but it is specifically used within IT to complement ITIL and other process disciplines in the achievement of an end result. As such, both Six Sigma and ITIL can coexist within an overall framework of control such as ISO/IEC 20000 and the EFQM Excellence Model, which is described next.

The EFQM Excellence Model

The EFQM Excellence Model, as already described in Chapter 1, is the most universally defined standard for world-class achievement, backed up by assessment and recognition processes that can be applied across Europe. The overall scope of the Excellence Model is reproduced in Figure 4.2.

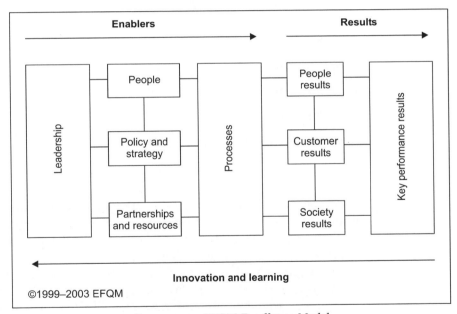

FIGURE 4.2 *EFQM Excellence Model*

Using the Excellence Model as a QMS is a way of ensuring that the widest possible view is taken of how an organization intends to approach quality. The Excellence Model can act as a host framework for ISO 9000, ISO/IEC 20000 and other standards that address specific aspects of IT delivery but that, on their own, cannot provide the whole picture. The Excellence Model provides a mix of perceptual and performance measures in nine different categories, which overall make up the operating scope of the organization. An IT department using such a model will be able to define its strategies and record its achievements in a repeatable way, without having to constantly refer back to proprietary processes that may no longer represent best practice. As can be seen, the model consists of nine primary criteria, each of which carries a weighting that contributes to the overall attainment. The weighting of each of the nine criteria of the Excellence Model in Figure 4.2 is shown here:

Enablers

Leadership	10%
People	9%
Policy and strategy	8%
Partnerships and resources	9%
Processes	14%
	50%

Results

People results	9%
Customer results	20%
Society results	6%
Key performance results	15%
	50%

It is now appropriate to provide a definition of each of these criteria and to show how they can be addressed by an organization using the Excellence Model as its primary QMS. Table 4.2 describes the detail of each of the nine criteria and the 32 sub-criteria that make them up.

The weighting system for the 32 sub-criteria is included in the scoring mechanism used to assess the position reached and uses more complex logic than can be covered in this book. Assessors, whether these are internal staff undertaking facilitation for self-assessment or external consultants performing an assessment as, say, preparation for submission for a Quality Award, need to be trained formally to perform the analysis properly; more information on assessment strategies as well as information on deployment of the Excellence Model can be found at www.bqf.org.uk.

TABLE 4.2 *The 9 criteria and 32 sub-criteria of the EFQM Excellence Model*

Criterion	Sub-criteria	
1 Leadership: how leaders develop and facilitate the achievement of the mission and vision, develop values required for long-term success and implement these via appropriate actions and behaviours, and are personally involved in ensuring the organization's management system is developed and implemented.	A.	Leaders develop the mission, vision and values, and are role models of a culture of excellence.
	B.	Leaders are personally involved in ensuring the organization's management system is developed, implemented and continuously improved.
	C.	Leaders are involved with customers, partners and representatives of society.
	D.	Leaders motivate, recognize and support the organization's people.
2 Policy and strategy: how the organization implements its mission and vision via a clear stakeholder-focused strategy, supported by relevant policies, plans, objectives, targets and processes.	A.	Policy and strategy are based on the present and future needs and expectations of stakeholders.
	B.	Policy and strategy are based on information from performance measurement, research, learning and creativity-related activities.
	C.	Policy and strategy are developed, reviewed and updated.
	D.	Policy and strategy are deployed through a framework of key processes.
	E.	Policy and strategy are communicated and implemented.
3 People: how the organization manages, develops and releases the full potential of its people at individual, team-based and organization-wide levels, and plans these activities in order to support its policy and strategy and the effective operation of its processes.	A.	People resources are planned, managed and improved.
	B.	People's knowledge and competencies are identified, developed and sustained.
	C.	People are involved and empowered.
	D.	People and the organization have a dialogue.
	E.	People are rewarded, recognized and cared for.
4 Partnerships and resources: how the organization plans and manages its external partnerships and internal resources in order to support its policy and strategy and the effective operation of its processes.	A.	External partnerships are managed.
	B.	Finances are managed.
	C.	Buildings, equipment and materials are managed.
	D.	Technology is managed.
	E.	Information and knowledge are managed.
5 Processes: how the organization designs, manages and improves its processes in order to support its policy and strategy and fully satisfy, and generate increasing value for, its customers and other stakeholders.	A.	Processes are systematically designed and managed.
	B.	Processes are improved, as needed, using innovation in order to fully satisfy and generate increasing value for customers and other stakeholders.
	C.	Products and services are designed and developed based on customer needs and expectations.
	D.	Products and services are produced, delivered and serviced.
	E.	Customer relationships are managed and enhanced.
6 Customer results: what the organization is achieving in relation to its external customers.	A.	Perception measures: overall image, products and services, sales and after-sales support and loyalty.
	B.	Performance indicators: overall image, products and services, sales and after-sales support and loyalty.
7 People results	A.	Perception measures: motivation and satisfaction.
	B.	Performance indicators: achievements, motivation and involvement, satisfaction and services provided to the organization's people.
8 Society results: what the organization is achieving in relation to local, national and international society as appropriate.	A.	Perception measures: performance as a responsible citizen, involvement in the communities where it operates, activities to reduce and prevent nuisance and harm from its operations and/or throughout the lifecycle of its products and reporting on activities to assist in the preservation and sustainability of resources.
	B.	Performance indicators: handling changes in employment levels, press coverage, dealings with authorities and accolades and awards received.
9 Key performance results: what the organization is achieving in relation to its planned performance.	A.	Key performance outcomes (lag): financial (share price, dividends, gross margin, net profit, sales, meeting of budgets) and non-financial (market share, time to market, volumes, success rates).
	B.	Key performance indicators (lead): processes, external resources including partnerships, financial, buildings, equipment and materials, technology, information and knowledge.

© 1999–2003 EFQM

It has already been explained that the scoring is out of 1000 points and that world-class results can start to be identified from 600 points and upwards, with European Quality award winners typically returning about 650 points or higher. It is usual for an initial assessment to return much lower scores, in the order of 300 or less, since it is unlikely that most IT organizations will take such an holistic view of their achievements as described by this model. From the weightings given to the different criteria, it can be seen which aspects offer the most potential for beneficial change, although the level of interdependency is such that a development made in one criterion may well flow though to some of the other criteria as well.

Examples of developments in the nine major criteria

The author has implemented changes to the management of a number of IT departments based on the EFQM Excellence Model and has been able to demonstrate sustainable improvements as a consequence. Some examples of the types of strategy deployed in each of the nine key criteria are shown here.

(1) Leadership:
- The establishment of *performance circles*, ad-hoc gatherings of people interested in particular topics, to address known and obviously manifest shortcomings. Such an approach will lead to significant change because the people involved are those who are most affected by the issue under review.
- The establishment of regular staff engagement sessions where top management visits individual teams in situ to assess results and solve practical issues in relation to strategy as perceived 'on the ground'.

(2) Policy and strategy:
- Development of a customer-centric engagement model to replace a technology systems-centric approach.
- Commitment to achieve a 15 per cent improvement in results year on year.

(3) People:
- Deployment of a recognized industry standard career and skills-planning model leading to the Investor in People (IIP) award.
- Investigation of all turnover, sick absence and underlying attitudes.

(4) Partnerships and resources:
- Engagement of specialists to benchmark IT operations and systems.
- Establishment of a centrally managed resource management system to prioritize staff contributions and communicate the different initiatives and dependencies to all IT people, including contractors.

(5) Processes:
- Deployment of ITIL for service delivery and service support.
- Development of an information security management system (ISMS) based on BS 7799.
- Achievement of ISO 9002 for operational service delivery.

(6) Customer results:
- Establishment of customer surveys for all grades of client personnel.
- Replacement of conventional SLAs with business-target-driven IT services.

(7) People results:
- Establishment of staff surveys for all grades of IT personnel.
- Institution of regular and frequent staff communication sessions.

(8) Society results:
- Achievement of specific industry awards and external recognition.
- Engagement with local communities through the donation of time, equipment and provision of expertise.

(9) Key performance results:
- Defining and achieving class-leading measures for productivity, efficiency and effectiveness.
- Elimination of non-value-adding work based on customer needs.

It can be seen from these examples that the Excellence Model does not exist in isolation. This is a major strength that underpins its value as a framework – for a QMS should not preclude the deployment of specific solutions in any of the criteria. In this regard, ISO 9000, ITIL, ISO/IEC 20000, ISO 17799 and other industry-strength standards can – and should – be used to address particular areas, although it is hoped by now that the context for deploying such standards and the likely contribution they can make will be better understood by looking at the overall business performance potential.

THE IT INFRASTRUCTURE LIBRARY

The ITIL is the defacto framework that documents best practices in IT service management. ITIL was originally developed in the 1980s through sponsorship by the Central Computer and Telecommunications Agency (CCTA), and the UK government has retained ownership ever since in the guise of the OGC. It is not, however, a framework that is specific to government and it is certainly not a standard that applies only to the UK. ITIL is a truly international standard that is applicable to commercial organizations as well as to government bodies and much of the content has been written by experts from the IT industry across the world. As a result, ITIL is the most widely accepted approach to service management and has supplanted many of the proprietary methods used by specialist consultancies. ITIL is extremely relevant to IT departments. As the name implies, it is structured as a library of process definitions. This library can be represented as shown in Figure 4.3.

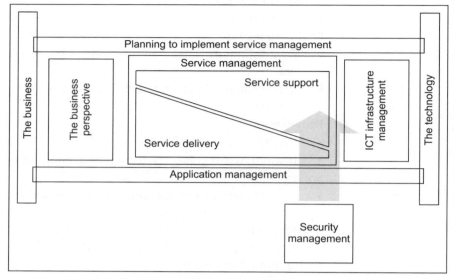

FIGURE 4.3   *ITIL publications framework*

There are numerous publications within the ITIL framework that document best practices, with those containing working definitions being as follows:

Service support	Describes processes for incident management, problem management, change management, release management, service desk and configuration management.
Service delivery	Describes processes for availability management, capacity management, financial management for IT services, service level management and IT service continuity management.
Application management	Describes the approach to the management of IT applications from the initial business need right through to systems retirement.
Security management	Describes the approach to the management of information security from an IT perspective.
ICT infrastructure management	Describes ICT infrastructure management from the identification of business requirements to the testing, installation and support of components and services.

There is clearly considerable overlap between the publications, as there is between the processes themselves. There are 13 processes that collectively make up the ITIL framework and that are capable of being defined and managed, 11 of them being covered by the service delivery and service support publications described above. These 11 processes are those most often deployed and where products and services are most frequently targeted. It can be seen that most of these processes are those used to discharge the requirements of ISO/IEC 20000, which reinforces the applicability of ITIL in any country. Many organizations regard the deployment of the 11 ITIL process definitions as an effective way of attaining best practice, although this is often not the end result – and this is not because the process definitions are wrong. What ITIL provides is a process definition, not an actual process operation, and the way in which processes are approached will make a huge difference to how well they run in practice. The author has discovered as many examples of ITIL processes being run badly as of non-ITIL processes being run well and the objective of any organization aspiring to be world-class has to be to adopt ITIL and establish levels of performance consistent with that aspiration. For example, if an IT department adopts a change management process based totally on ITIL, but cannot implement changes without an excessive lead time, then customers will not regard that IT department as world class – because it won't be. Practice and performance need to be aligned, which is why Chapter 8 describes world-class achievement metrics. What this chapter does, however, is to position ITIL as the underpinning process set that enables the consistent achievement of such performance levels so that organizations do not have to write their own.

The role of automation tools

Many software products are available that claim they are 'ITIL compatible', but this needs to be viewed with caution since what it means is that they can be used in a way suggested by ITIL, although of course they can also be used in different ways. The only products that are truly worthy of ITIL being used to support their marketing are those verified by independent agencies as being designed to work solely in an ITIL manner or that enforce the ITIL process definitions. An example of one such product is shown in Figure 4.4. A case study showing how it has been used in practice is described in the box that follows.

Figure 4.4 represents the Alignability Process Model, or Alignability™ for short, a software tool that has been designed to ensure that ITIL processes are adopted and that detailed work instructions are provided. This is essential because, although ITIL provides the guidelines, it does not define the processes at working levels – a book cannot enforce them, whereas a software tool can. This process management model provides specific, detailed instructions on how services should be delivered and supported, based on the latest ITIL guidelines. It can be used standalone or, to gain most benefit

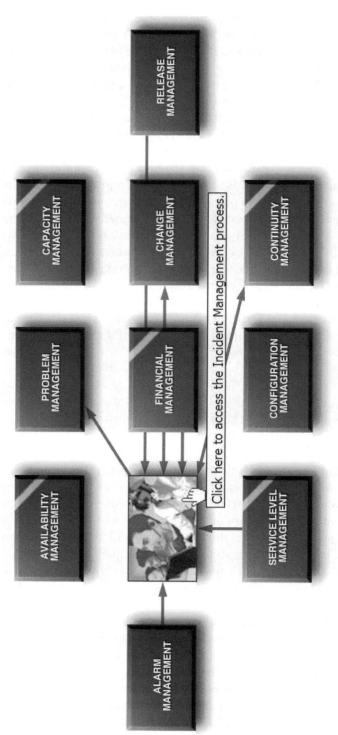

Click here to access the Incident Management process.

FIGURE 4.4 *Alignability Process Model*

from it, installed alongside a service management product such as HP Open-View Service Desk or Peregrine ServiceCenter, where it will configure the operation of these tools according to its predefined procedures and work instructions. It acts as an effective bridge between documented best practices such as ITIL and the operation of service management toolsets, making ITIL a repeatable and enforceable standard rather than a discretionary process. The representation in Figure 4.4 does not cover the full product features of Alignability, which is a registered trademark of Service Management Partners, Inc and which can be accessed at www.alignability.com.

CASE STUDY USING THE ALIGNABILITY PROCESS MODEL

The Medicines and Healthcare Products Regulatory Agency (MHRA) resulted from the merger of the Medicines Control Agency (MCA) and the Medical Devices Agency (MDA) and has as its primary objective the protection and promotion of public health and patient safety by ensuring that medicines, healthcare products and medical equipment are safe for those who use them. The IT company running systems and infrastructure for the MHRA wanted to consolidate the services of the two merged organizations and to establish best practice based on ITIL definitions, especially for change, configuration and service level management, in an accelerated timescale, which meant that a conventional approach would not have met the deadline. Alignability™ was therefore applied to create processes and detailed work instructions for the following service elements:

- service definitions (service hours, business importance, configuration item (CI) structure, SLAs and details of provider responsibilities);
- support management;
- contact administration;
- configuration administration;
- root cause analysis;
- change management;
- service level management;
- roles and specialist support groups.

The work was completed in less than three months from start to finish, involving conversion of existing support information from the previous helpdesks, incorporation of the procedures into the helpdesk product that supported the MHRA – HP OpenView Service Desk – and implementation of all the operations management and reporting tools used to provide information. All the relevant staff were trained in the ITIL processes during the short project time, and the processes were published on the intranet. Alignability™ accelerated deployment of this solution many times beyond what could have been achieved by a manual deployment. Not only did this meet the business timescale, but it has also resulted in a service based on best-practice process definitions that are enforced by the tools being used.

It is this type of process enforcement that makes the difference between service delivery departments striving to achieve best practice and those that actually attain it. ITIL alone cannot achieve consistent results because human nature will find a way round any documented process, whereas ITIL enforced by a management system such as Alignability™ that automatically configures service management tools with procedures and work instructions to automate ITIL guidance is clearly sustainable, repeatable and means it warrants the defacto world-class process management system accolade. This is important for other reasons as well, since there is an increasing focus on governance in IT and there is an expectation that every element of IT will be able to demonstrate how it is controlled. Two frameworks that are used for such purposes are Capability Maturity Model Integration (CMMI), from the Software Engineering Institute of Carnegie Mellon University in the USA, and Control Objectives for Information Technology (CobiT), promoted by the IT Governance Institute, also based in the USA. These frameworks explain management control as conforming to one of five different maturity levels and they both use the same staged model, which provides strong credence to their applicability. Table 4.3 shows a representation of the five levels defined by CMMI and CobiT; and it can be seen that level 3 should be the minimum standard of attainment that an organization aspiring to be world class should strive to meet.

TABLE 4.3 *Representation of maturity model levels*

Maturity level	Staged representation maturity levels
1	Initial
2	Managed
3	Defined
4	Quantitatively managed
5	Optimizing

Organizations using CMMI to govern systems development will operate their development processes according to defined guidelines, and these offer both a relative and an absolute position to best practice. For an IS function, CMMI represents the development industry equivalent of ITIL, and it would be inappropriate to develop an accreditation track for one part of IT in isolation. Although best practice may be considered as having achieved level 5, this may only be appropriate for systems houses or third-party providers that make a living from product development, as opposed to the delivery and support of effective systems for commercial use.

In the experience of the author, level 3 is the minimum target level that defines attainment of best practice for in-house IT functions, and ITIL addresses this level. Products such as Alignability™ enable the achievement of level 4, which is a clear step forward from just having processes in place. CMMI and CobiT provide frameworks for benchmarking how well processes are being managed and, in the same way that products such as SAP and Oracle Financials introduce repeatability and compliance within a Finance function, so ITIL and Alignability™ provide the same framework within service delivery. CMMI, CobiT, ITIL and Alignability™ are all components of the overall world-class proposition for IT.

Alignability™ contains the latest ITIL process definitions within its operating model, and so IT staff do not need to consult the original publications after implementation. This also means that updates of Alignability™ will incorporate any future changes to ITIL definitions, which is particularly important in the context of sustainable investment. ITIL is unlikely to be a static definition and will continue to be developed and enhanced, so it should not be implemented in a way that inhibits its deployment.

Qualifications and accreditation

Having the ability to deploy best practice processes backed up by class-leading process management solutions inevitably places a great deal of emphasis on the understanding and capability of the service delivery staff who operate them. We saw in Chapter 3 that ISEB and EXIN offer accreditation for courses run by authorized training providers that teach how ITIL should be used, and the integrity of a QMS depends on the skills and attributes of the staff responsible for process deployment. Although tools such as Alignability™ will take away some of the detail of ITIL, anyone using them must know about the fundamentals, the terminology and the service intent that makes up each process definition. Becoming appropriately qualified is one way to demonstrate that the investment in a QMS is a serious endorsement of the likely end result.

OTHER POSSIBLE STANDARDS

There are a number of other standards that can also be applied to IT departments, but analysis of them has not been included here for the sake of simplicity. However, for completeness, these standards are CobiT 4.0, ISO 14000 covering environmental management, ISO 10007 for configuration management and ISO 17799 for security management. These are deployed less extensively, except in specialist IT organizations, although ISO 17799 is of particular interest to online service providers; as it can be used to satisfy the security requirements of ISO/IEC 20000, it is an important standard for service managers to consider. For this reason, ISO 17799 is covered in more detail in Chapter 7 on IT governance. CobiT 4.0 is a product of the IT Governance Institute (ITGI) in the USA and details of how to access the standard, as a free download, can be found at www.itgi.com.

SUMMARY

- Formal use of a QMS is essential to act as the controlling framework for management, reporting and user visibility.
- Thirty-two characteristics of quality are defined in the EFQM Excellence Model.
- Best-practice techniques should coexist and fit within the chosen QMS.
- ITIL and Six Sigma can enable externally validated improvements in results if deployed correctly and when aimed at the right problems.
- Automation is critical to ensure that processes are used consistently and that service management toolsets are used only in a defined manner.

5 Developing the business proposition

The techniques of investment appraisal have long been used in IT to evaluate the business benefits of spend on development projects, which are mostly regarded as value adding but are usually discretionary in nature. However, such techniques are rarely applied by IT services departments because the linkage between investment levels, return on investment (ROI) and the ongoing cost of delivery has not been articulated properly. This is a pity, because the benefits of formal appraisal will often yield as much value from careful investment in service capability as from yet another new product system. This chapter sets out the methods used to determine the economic value of discretionary investments, explains the context within which a business case should be presented and shows some real examples of service propositions that articulated – and delivered – their benefits successfully.

GAINING APPROVAL FOR THE BUSINESS CASE

An analysis, by a team involving the author, of over 2600 service projects in 550 different companies returned some surprising results. Over 75 per cent of these projects were completed in order to improve customer service, and yet only 12 per cent of them had yielded any form of financial benefit. Of course, not all projects will show a financial return, although it could be argued that the cost of poor service will lead to loss of custom and therefore addressing this concern will show a benefit – but the organizations concerned did not generally take this into account in their submissions. Many of these service improvement projects were felt to have some financial justification, although there was little or no evidence provided of a detailed, robust or consistent ROI process to demonstrate the value. Despite this, measurement of the value derived from these projects was seen to be important in 37 per cent of the companies surveyed.

The context for ROI

Investment appraisal is carried out in order to provide realistic estimates of the economic value of individual projects. In so doing, it will take into account both the costs and the benefits – in financial terms – over a set period, working on the cost of funds, the prevailing interest rates and any risk associated with realization of the claimed benefits. In a company with limited access to funds, either for capital borrowing or by drawing from reserves depending on its liquidity status, all projects need to compete against each other for management consideration. The main purpose of any investment decision is to obtain an ROI greater than the initial outlay. As most projects will take some time to deliver the intended return, account must be taken of the changing value of money because £1000 benefit in five years' time will not have the same value as £1000 today. This is taken into account by means of a discounted cash flow (DCF) approach, which converts the future benefits and costs to a common date using either net present value (NPV) or an internal rate of return (IRR). Although this may seem complex, the process is simplified by means of standard accounting routines used by most finance departments and, in reality, you need to provide a surprisingly small amount of information – but it has to be accurate and it has to yield an attractive benefit, otherwise the exercise is pointless. NPV applies a rate of discount based on the marginal cost of funds for future cash flows to rebase them back to the present day. The figure used will depend on the rate at which your organization can access funds, which will fluctuate with both the base rate and the company's external credit rating, as determined by agencies, such as Standard & Poor's and Moody's, which banks consult when making lending decisions.

WORKED EXAMPLE

The way in which NPV is calculated is by use of the formula for compound interest, which is worked backwards to provide a present value for a future benefit based on the notional rate of interest at which you borrow funds:

$$P = \frac{\text{benefit}}{(1+r)^n}$$

where P is the present value, r is the interest rate and n is the time period

So, if we wish to achieve a benefit of £16,000 in year 5, this benefit will represent £11,956 in today's value terms assuming an annual rate of interest of 6 per cent. This can be demonstrated as follows:

$$P = \frac{£16,000}{(1 + 0.06)^5} = £11,956$$

So let's assume that you can invest your company's funds at 6 per cent for the next five years in a bank or use the same funds to pay for a proposed project. To find out whether your project is worthwhile, we need to adjust the returns achieved by your project by the interest rate we could get by the 'safe' option and use this discount rate to modify both costs and benefits. If a service improvement project costs £100,000 in year 1 and returns an annual benefit stream of £25,000 for the next four years, then would such an investment be worthwhile? To decide this, we adjust the cash flows – investment and returns – by the interest rate, which will yield, in this example, discount factors of 0.943 in year 1, 0.899 in year 2, 0.839 in year 3, 0.792 in year 4 and 0.747 in year 5. Calculating the NPV for this project means multiplying the investment level by 0.943 and then adding in the subsequent year's benefits multiplied by the respective discount factors. In this example, the NPV result is negative at −£12,375, meaning that the returns achieved by your project are worse than investing the money in a bank.

You can make a better case either by spreading out the investment over more than one year or by seeking to get either more benefits or achieving them sooner. It is best to do this before you seek formal approval, because having a project refused once does not bode well for getting it evaluated again.

Of course, having a positive NPV does not show you what the actual ROI is. This figure, the IRR, is calculated by finding the rate of investment earned throughout the life of the project. Let's assume that you have adjusted the benefits achieved by your project from £25,000 to £30,000 in years 2 to 5, which now gives an NPV of £4010. This is a positive result, which will be attractive to your accountants, but what does it mean in terms of return on investment? This is calculated in reverse by using the formula to achieve an NPV of zero – in other words, what the ROI needs to be in order to break even compared with interest rates. So, if a company can borrow funds at less than the internal rate of return from your project, then you stand a better chance of getting investment approval. IRR can also be used to differentiate between two competing investment proposals with different cash flows, since the overall value would be used as the decision criterion and not the effect in any single year. In our example, the IRR becomes 7.75 per cent and this can usefully be regarded as representing the ROI.

Most companies will establish a hurdle rate below which investments are not considered viable. This is because of the risk associated with the return of benefits in future years and also to help focus attention on projects with a high, rather than a mediocre, rate of return. Typical hurdle rates can be as low as 15 per cent or as high as 50 per cent, with 100 per cent sometimes used when a company wants all of its projects to pay back within one year, although this is unusual. Sophisticated investment appraisal models will also take account of expected future interest rates based on economic intelligence, and so the maths can become complicated – but IT people cope well with complexity!

EXAMINATION OF SOME SERVICE TRANSFORMATION PROJECTS

In order to counter the potentially negative survey information shown at the start of this chapter, a number of service success stories are outlined here.

CASE STUDY – A HIGH-STREET BANK

Let's take a look at a business case that established a new helpdesk for a high-street bank. This organization wanted to consolidate a number of separate helpdesks and at the same time increase the capability of its staff to answer customer IT queries, which could originate from counter staff, head-office functions and corporate clients. The benefits from this were seen as a reduction in internal costs by being able to handle more calls at first touch, which is cheaper than getting technical specialists involved, and by handling calls faster by use of a knowledge base containing the solutions to previously reported problems.

The total authorized cost of the project was £2.1 million, consisting of workstations, furniture, helpdesk software and all other project development costs such as relocation and staff training. Using a cost of funds of 10.5 per cent and an evaluation period of five years yielded an NPV of +£404,000, with an IRR of 17.5 per cent. This was an attractive proposition that was approved on financial grounds, although of course what it also delivered was a standard of service that increased first-time fix rates to 80 per cent and that also yielded a commensurate improvement in customer satisfaction ratings. If a lower figure was used for the cost of funds based on more favourable interest rates, then this project would have returned an even better result, thus illustrating the fact that the same operational benefits could have been delivered for the same cost but with a higher NPV and better IRR – so investment timing is critical.

Other examples of successful service improvement projects that can be outlined here are:

- the move to a process-based organization model from a previous hierarchical silo model that returned 27.6 per cent and an NPV of +£2.05 million;
- a distributed systems management regime for several thousand PC workstations that achieved a 71.6 per cent payback with an NPV of +£2.29 million;
- an enterprise management scheme that consolidated three data centres into one, delivering an IRR of 30 per cent with an NPV of +£2.72 million, and introduced automated alerting and single-point operations capability.

None of these projects was undertaken solely for financial reasons, but the combination of improved service quality allied to quantifiably lower costs of delivery made the project propositions more compelling than would have been the case otherwise.

Benefits realization

Once approval has been given to make the investment in service improvement, it is crucial to ensure the claimed benefits are delivered. Not only is this important for the project itself, but it also ensures a level of credibility with your accountants for when you next raise a project proposal. The standard way to do this is by means of a post-implementation review (PIR) that analyses the claimed benefits and costs versus the actual achievements. Of course, this presumes that the costs and benefits are tracked throughout the project, and, although this is an essential management discipline, it is one that is sometimes overlooked.

In the helpdesk case study above, the PIR yielded an IRR of 29.6 per cent and an NPV of +£720,000 because opportunities to deliver benefits earlier were taken by the project manager, the capital costs were lower than estimated due to good supplier negotiation, and fewer people than expected needed to relocate. Of course, it is not always the case that claimed benefits can be bettered, but it is essential to track the project carefully in order to spot potential problems earlier and to show the progress.

One way of ensuring benefits realization is to publish the targets at project inception and revisit them regularly through the project life, using an external specialist – say, an accountant – to work the figures for you. This provides a degree of credibility to the claims you make for such benefits as well as ensuring that the right figures are used at the right time. Of critical importance, however, to the perceived success of any service improvement project is the customer experience, which needs to be measured at the start of the project and then again once it has finished. Being able to quantify service benefits will ensure customer support for future initiatives.

So we have seen that making a business case for a service improvement project is much the same as any other form of discretionary investment. The key differences between systems and services projects are in the management mindset, and, once these are overcome, the rest is straightforward. Some key conclusions can be drawn from this:

- Be able to identify tangible benefits as well as the initial investment.
- Find out the hurdle rate and other financial targets in your company.
- Be able to quantify customer benefits in financial and service terms.
- Use a spreadsheet to model the effect of different project scenarios.
- Be as business-minded in service delivery as the systems department.

UPTIME VERSUS CUSTOMER SATISFACTION – THE CONFLICT

Figure 3.6 in Chapter 3 showed the service delivery value chain as perceived by the customer and, differently, by a typical silo-based IT department. This situation is commonplace, but clearly the service view is the one that carries most weight since it is increasingly the case that the voice of the customer is the one that matters most. This is because the customers not only have a commercial veto over whose services they use but they are also increasingly operating the IT infrastructure of the service provider themselves rather than being a passive recipient of operations management delivered through a customer service intermediary. The explosion in the number and types of service being delivered online, either exclusively or in tandem with conventional channels, means that most businesses can no longer rely on intermediation by customer service departments – the person in the street transacts with the company through the mechanism of the IT infrastructure. This could equally well be a department of central or local government providing information and access to services, a commercial organization servicing products and orders, a membership body serving the information and professional needs of its subscribers, or a charity collecting donations for a major crisis appeal. Whatever the remit of the organization, today's service expectations are that the majority of work will be done online. This is not only a case of providing a useable web interface – consumers and professionals alike expect to transact business in a number of different ways that include fulfilment capability, which means linking the browser dialogue to core systems. Online transaction processing by customers is not straightforward from a service delivery perspective for several reasons:

- The transaction paths involve more handoffs between different systems than services designed for customer clerks to operate.
- Performance management needs to take account of factors that are not under the direct control of the operations and network teams.
- Frequency and duration of access are at the customer's discretion.
- Access to the IT helpdesk is required in the event of difficulty, and this will be split equally between performance and 'how can I?' issues.
- There will be increased emphasis on authentication, non-repudiation and the origin of transactions that lie outside corporate boundaries.

These factors can expose an underlying weakness in corporate IT infrastructures, which may prevent a satisfactory external customer experience unless addressed. Figure 5.1 exemplifies a typical service delivery infrastructure

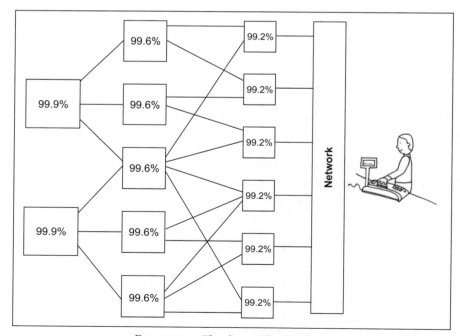

FIGURE 5.1   *The downside of uptime*

scenario, with annual service-availability figures included for the different principal elements.

The traditional emphasis of high database-server availability means a lot less in a consumer transaction than it has in the past. More application, network, authentication, routing and web servers are needed to serve a consumer than a customer clerk on the corporate local-area network (LAN) and so the intrinsic availability will be arithmetically lower – a typical internet banking application may need as many as 250 different servers in order to deliver the service. Yet there is a paradox that the service availability expected by the consumer will be greater than that expected by the customer clerk, because once a service is offered online, many of the restrictions over use of that service are no longer applicable without disenfranchising the public. Building a service for true 24×7 availability is not the same as building a service for week-day office hours, and different approaches are needed.

Single points of failure

Any good systems design will take account of what happens in the event of a core component becoming unavailable. A world-class systems design servicing consumers will always take account of component availability and provide alternative routing and either – or both – online and in-person help-desk facilities. Consideration of single points of failure will be not only for the network components but also for the application servers, database and people elements that make up the end-to-end experience, and many of these components will need to manage themselves in real time. By self-management, we are referring to automated failover methods, whereby any service component is shadowed by another; by load balancing, that a peak workload on one component is shared by another without technical intervention; and by self-healing, that a failed transaction is diagnosed and repaired, and transaction performance is managed within a range of limits rather than left to chance. All these elements of the consumer delivery chain place far more emphasis on the service management regime than centrally run systems where operators track throughput on performance monitors.

A world-class transaction-processing system designed for consumer use should be looking to return 99.995 per cent uptime measured across a 365-day year. As we saw in Chapter 4, this level of availability equates to just over 26 minutes of unavailability a year, and even this should be notified to customers in advance wherever possible. Some consumers do pay their gas bills and check their current accounts online on Christmas Day – and expect such services to be available just because their ISP is available. This expectation demands a lot from a company that normally trades only week-day hours and is certainly not confined only to online concerns.

SERVICE QUALITY PERCEPTION

Another important aspect of the service delivery chain is that of perceived quality. A bad customer experience on one occasion generates a poor impression of the service provider; two consecutive bad experiences can lead to formal complaints or a move of business elsewhere, even if the online service is better than was previously provided by that company through its customer service function. This is primarily because the service expectation is higher when the customer is transacting electronically and also because the customer is interacting with system rules that allow no service discretion, unlike a service agent who can authorize something out of limits if the customer transaction warrants it. Designing automated systems to provide a level of discretion is remarkably difficult, and yet the consumer will perceive a problem with the service if he or she is blocked from carrying out a reasonable request just because the system rules do not cater for it. Best practice in service design, as has been discussed already, takes a representative account of consumer-activity patterns when building an online service, and this has to cater for disabled as well as able customers. Incorporation of customer expectations and capabilities into a new service design to cater for these aspects is important. The following table shows typical customer reactions when a service becomes unavailable:

Service level attainment	Customer reaction
Below 90%	Inform the media
90–95%	Write to the industry regulator
95–97.5%	Write to the company chairperson
97.5–99%	Contact the complaints department
99–99.75%	It's OK, I suppose . . .
Above 99.75%	My minimum expectation

The reason this is perceived quality is a simple one – no actual SLA will exist with the customer, and so there is no measurement standard against which delivery can be assessed. The only measure of relevance is the attitude of the customer to the loss of availability, which for competitive services often results in a direct loss of business, as seen in Chapter 4, and for tied services where the consumer needs something specific from their supplier, be that a bank or a utility company, often results in a complaint. Here we also see a different scenario emerging, because the recipient of the complaint is often not the IT department itself; nor does the complaint always get directed at the company, and the media publish many examples of high-profile service failures that do not get handled through conventional internal incident and problem-management processes. This is because the consumer rarely has the means to make contact with the IT infrastructure team, and often the customer service department that they do contact is unable to intermediate because the department is not aware of whether the IT service is operational, or what to do about it. So this leads to a complaint aimed at the organizational level – from the chairperson right through to the complaints department, if one exists, or to the media or industry regulator if not. Consumers are remarkably intolerant of service unavailability, and because, they don't work in the same company as the person to whom they are complaining, can often be abusive or aggressive.

The helpdesk scenario

The number of complaints logged has often been used as a means of service acceptance, although this is no longer regarded as the best measure of how well a service is performing. The only complaints that are logged are those that are received through conventional channels, and reading about a service scenario that has affected your own organization in the weekly trade press does not constitute a complaint in such terms. Emerging best practice in this regard is the number of accolades received for good service and, although this is hard to orchestrate, the results can be remarkable. The positive impact of someone experiencing a problem and for it being handled in an unexpected way will lead to an expression of delight rather than one of grudging acceptance, such as the case of a woman who reported a problem with a cash machine, only for the branch manager to turn up on her doorstep with her card and the money she had been trying to withdraw. Such events are a manifestation of service excellence not of service level agreements and, in an online world, percentage service-attainment figures are no longer the norm, having been replaced with responsiveness figures in the unlikely event of outage. Such responsiveness figures are measured in minutes rather than hours and should lead to solutions being put in place in order to prevent the future recurrence of avoidable problems. This is what the ITIL process for problem management exists to provide, but many companies treat each incident on its own and deliver a level of service geared at solving the incident rather than resolving the underlying problem. This can best be illustrated by looking at IT helpdesk call profiles as shown in Figures 5.2 and 5.3. These are actual examples and are typical of many helpdesks that the author reviews in the course of his work.

The profile in Figure 5.2 shows that the helpdesk receives a peak of calls around 9 am, lasting until 10 am, when the call volume drops significantly. It then picks up again at 2 pm before progressively tailing off throughout the afternoon. As a one-off event, this could be regarded as the result of a particular issue with one service in one location; however, when this scenario is repeated the next day, and the day after that, this is obviously not the case, and Figure 5.3 from a different organization in a different service sector illustrates the point – which is especially relevant since the company whose

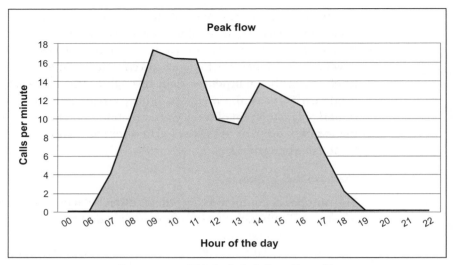

FIGURE 5.2 *IT helpdesk daily call profile*

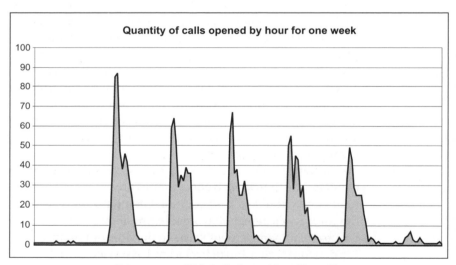

FIGURE 5.3 *IT helpdesk weekly call profile*

profile generated Figure 5.2 also had the same day-of-week profile as that shown in Figure 5.3.

Figures 5.2 and 5.3 display a remarkable fact about the current state of IT delivery: both organizations enjoyed a perception from their management that their helpdesks were good performers because they were dealing with a large number of incidents within short call-handling times. They were also achieving low call-waiting and abandonment rates, and so as far as the operational perception measures were concerned, no changes were expected. However, when the customers of those service providers were contacted, there was a very different story – they felt the IT organizations were not solving the real underlying problems and resented having to ring the helpdesk, even if they did admit that the responsiveness was good. This was exacerbated as both service providers charged for calls made to the helpdesk, which, given that most of the faults being reported were under the control of IT, left a poor perception of value and a reluctance to ring the helpdesk. This might result not only in faults not being corrected but in interim solutions being provided by the 'back door' without being recorded and hence not being seen as part of the overall quality of service.

This type of call profile generates a number of significant implications:

- Call resolution and not call prevention is the defacto measure of service effectiveness. However, preventing the need for calls is a better service proposition than simply handling them within tight time-scales.
- Incident handling is done on the basis of repetition, not intuition.
- Helpdesk staff are needed to handle faults that IT themselves create.
- Peak call volumes at critical times of day, which is when customers are trying to do their own jobs but can't, will reduce productivity.
- Root cause analysis is not being given sufficient priority in the firm.

Establishing a problem-management function with a mandate to reduce the total number of calls as well as to analyse and resolve the daily call peaks takes remarkably few human resources but delivers significant perceptual benefit. Eliminating the need to call a helpdesk means the service is running as it was designed to do and the customer is being as productive as they are capable of being – which might not be good enough, but this will be covered separately in Chapter 6. An organization with a low incidence of helpdesk calls but potentially worse resolution times invariably has a lower cost profile than one that has headline incident-management statistics, because that company is investing in service excellence and not helpdesk-management excellence. The issue about time to resolve should be dependent on the class of service that is being delivered, with high numbers of repetitive problems having been eliminated, meaning that the few remaining problems are those worthy of closer and more detailed attention.

Resolving calls and not just answering them

The next issue to be addressed once the call volumes and call-handling processes have been managed properly is that of call-resolution timescales. Although operationally it looks good if there is a fast time to answer, it is of little service relevance if a fix cannot be delivered in a timely manner. Best practice in this regard is that 80 per cent of requests for assistance should be resolved within the period of the initial telephone call, which should not be longer than about two minutes; beyond that, desk-side support should be invoked. An analogy used here is that of a roadside rescue request, where someone who is a member of a motoring organization calls for help in the event of a breakdown. The operator carries out a number of checks with the distressed driver and then schedules a recovery vehicle response if the problem cannot be diagnosed and cannot be resolved by the driver within the first few minutes. As the response time for the recovery vehicle may average 45 minutes, the elapsed time before the driver gets an appropriate intervention gets worse the longer a dialogue with the operator continues. It is good IT practice to decide whether to invoke desk-side support within that first 2-minute period and for support to be provided to users on main corporate sites within 15 minutes – and for a fix to be provided and the call closed without further user involvement within 30 minutes. For users on remote sites, the time to resolve may extend to between two and four hours, depending on how remote the location is, with eight hours probably representing the maximum time to fix. This applies similarly to consumer IT issues, where next-day on-site support is becoming the norm and for the same reasons – the expectation of responsiveness has to match the degree to which that service is regarded as essential to daily life.

Service responsiveness

Although good fix-on-fail results will result in a good perception of the help-desk, the satisfaction of new work requests is also one of the real tests of IT service orientation. Best-practice companies will deliver 100 per cent of their commitments within an agreed timescale, and 95 per cent of new installations will be completed within 72 hours of the request being made – including delivery of a new piece of hardware, any necessary software and the network changes required to bring them into service. A new facility should also be commissioned by one empowered individual rather than a series of different individuals – the more people attending a customer installation, the worse the customer perception of IT becomes – and rightly so, because highly silo-driven service providers are usually the least efficient. What this means inside a typical corporate organization is a different management structure, whereby customer service delivery is part of the operations remit and not separate from it, in order to enforce good operational disciplines as well as good provision. Network teams may be reluctant to cede responsibility for network changes to a PC installation technician, although modern patch-management systems are designed to allow relatively unskilled (in telecommunications terms) staff to do this safely. The skill levels in the tele-communications team should be more about design, strategy, tariff control and network management, and less about employing people to use patch leads – an installation technician can follow rules if those rules are explained properly.

IT generally does not enjoy a particularly good reputation when it comes to change management. There are few things that concern customers more than when a long-awaited change is implemented, only for it to fail – or at the very least, not do what it was supposed to do. It is imperative to measure and report on change management activities in order to focus attention on getting it right first time, on time and every time. A traditional approach to change management often involves having so many individuals in the approval chain that no-one really feels accountable, and this can extend the timescales beyond what customers believe to be reasonable. A better approach becomes possible once a good systems management framework is put in place that allows configurations to be recorded and examined remotely and for changes to be targeted at known and specific elements – which is especially relevant for those elements servicing the customer directly. Establishing these types of framework is typically part of how software companies such as Microsoft and Symantec understand what software each workstation known to them contains and what it needs in terms of updates or changes, and the success rate in applying these changes is extremely high. Commercial organizations aiming for world-class status should base their change management regime on a number of fundamental components:

- a configuration management database (CMDB) that records all the configuration items (CIs) that make up a customer service: this CMDB will hold the definitive record of every item, and its key attributes, in a way that is accessible to both the helpdesk and operations management systems of which change management is a key component;
- discovery and tracking tools that 'find' assets connected to the network and allow these to be recorded as CIs;
- systems frameworks that allow configuration changes to be made online and checked against the original specification on implementation;
- a backout plan, so if anything goes wrong, it can be reversed rapidly;
- a clear definition of what has to be managed as a change and what does not – for example, auto-updating virus signatures would normally be exempted from the change regime because this activity is operating in a prescribed and tightly controlled manner and has already been tested. This type of activity is generally known as a preauthorized change; the stronger the management framework, the greater the number of preauthorized changes that can be sanctioned;
- applications can also be included in the scope of a CMDB.

The net result of an effective management regime based on the above attributes is that changes happen more quickly, with a much higher chance of success and involving fewer people than a conventional paper-based approach. A change success rate of 99.5 per cent or better and an overall change implementation cycle of three days or less is typical in world-class companies.

The pitfalls of case studies

There are a number of case studies in this book that describe real-life service transformation examples, and these have been included to make the concepts being discussed more tangible. They are often regarded as the most helpful way of explaining the results of a service improvement project and yet few finance directors regard them as relevant – which can be a potential problem. The reasons for this are quite diverse and are outlined here, together with some advice on how to approach published case studies based on the five most often encountered reasons for rejecting them:

- **Reason 1:** 'They've been written by a supplier to put their offering in the best possible light, and the example chosen does not represent what can be achieved normally.'

  This critique is potentially valid, and a reputable supplier should be able to offer a number of case studies covering a range of examples, rather than a single flagship project. It is entirely reasonable for a supplier to want to promote the success of a company that has generated significant benefits from using its product or service, and the principle of *caveat emptor* – 'buyer beware' – applies in all such cases. Case studies should be approached with normal commercial caution.

- **Reason 2:** 'They are written from a supplier's perspective and do not represent what the customer actually achieved.'

  This critique is unusual nowadays because the penalties for misrepresenting the capabilities of a product or service are quite severe. English law contains many remedies for product claims, including prosecution by the Advertising Standards Agency. Although some case studies cannot be attributed to the client organization for publicity reasons, they still have to be truthful, and no-one would be advised to take case study benefits as representative of what they could achieve without some form of customer validation if a supplier claim is used.

- **Reason 3:** 'The customer example is not relevant in our line of business.'

  Although this certainly can be true, the management of IT does not contain as much variability as businesspeople believe. The techniques and methods referenced in this book have been used in every industry sector and have delivered the same results – the only variability is the way in which the projects were managed. If IT was unique to each type of industry, then there would be no outsourcing industry; nor could there be generic best-practice techniques. Some aspects of IT will be industry-specific – for example, cash machines are used only in financial services, but the way in which they are managed can be used to equal effect in eticketing machines for airlines and train operating companies.

- **Reason 4:** 'The best case studies are years old and so may be out of date.'

  It can take time to establish and publicize a transformation project, especially one that is perceived to deliver competitive advantage. By the time a case study reaches the wider market, the organization inevitably will have moved on – but the point is whether the approach taken is relevant for your organization at the time it was undertaken. A company good enough to be used as a case study will be well on the way to best practice, and it is quite likely that its experience will help your organization address the issue that the case study company has already solved.

- **Reason 5:** 'The case study involves a competitor and it is inappropriate to seek their advice on how they achieved the published result.'

    This is a common problem, and one to which the supplier will also be sensitive because of commercial confidentiality issues. However, most sectors are represented by some form of best-practice forum or users' association where it is common to share experiences, even with competitors, on the basis of professional networking. This informal exchange of views does not extend to the exchange of privileged information, but it does put any case study in perspective and paints a picture of how much the supplier did as opposed to how much the client organization achieved under its own leadership. Networking organizations such as The Corporate IT Forum (.tif), which represents corporate IT interests within a supplier-free membership, and the IT Infrastructure Forum (itSMF), which exists exclusively to serve the service management industry, are two examples where best practices and project examples can be shared without commercial conflict or contractual bars.

SUMMARY

- Use the same financial appraisal techniques for service improvement projects as you would for systems development projects.
- Use post-implementation reviews (PIRs) as a means of formalizing the benefits that a service transformation project has achieved.
- Manage issues of service perception at least as much as tangible results.
- Aim to deliver results that show improvement in responsiveness as well as any cost, quality and functional measures.
- Treat case studies as a valuable resource and validate them through networking organizations that help members to share best practice.

6 Redefining the role of the user

Many of the chapters in this book concentrate on the changes needed within service delivery in order to generate best practices, but they all allude to the fact that service is a cooperative rather than a one-way transaction. Service quality is as good as the customer wants it to be, and the customer's behaviour can influence this quite significantly, regardless of whether they are aware of it. Most of us have witnessed the 'customer-from-hell' syndrome and felt sympathy for the person trying to offer help in an impossible situation; equally, most of us have experienced the 'stupid-company' scenario as described by the National Consumer Council report mentioned in the introduction to this book, where the company seems to go to endless lengths to ruin whatever reputation it might have had in the first place. It is no different in the world of IT service delivery than it is in any other service scenario, and increasingly we live in a service economy that demands customer management skills. This chapter, therefore, uncovers a number of techniques that are especially relevant to the management of customer perception and competency in the operation of IT and that are essential for the accession of service delivery to best practice and then world class.

THE DIFFERENCES BETWEEN A USER AND A CUSTOMER

An IT service user can be defined as someone who is provided with a service that they have not themselves been party to the specification of. A user will typically be someone in a corporate or consumer environment using systems designed and programmed by IT specialists, who will, we hope, have taken account of the customer's needs when designing an IT service. This is the classical definition of a user – someone who uses what they are given and no more – and we have become used to treating users with an element of disdain. This is unfortunate, because users are actually people who have less scope for engagement with the IT organization and therefore least to lose from being obnoxious when something goes wrong. Users are amorphous, unseen and unknown and often treated by IT as generic problems, sitting in a helpdesk queue awaiting their turn to be served. When the user is connected, he or she is usually managed under a regime of minimum time spent on the problem and a solution based on the Pareto principle – 80 per cent of the problems can be solved by 20 per cent of the possible available solutions. It is this level of service user who holds the worst view of service delivery because they are managed on a least-cost basis, often from overseas and on the basis that the issue about which they are calling is one to be solved and not resolved. What can be done for this class of customer is to provide a level of service that meets the customer's needs and also probably exceeds their initial expectations. If someone expects little then they will respond well to being treated as an individual, and world-class helpdesks operate to high productivity levels while retaining a degree of customer care and engagement. They do this by following a few simple but meaningful techniques:

- establishment of recorded welcome messages based on known events – such as 'We are aware of the virus outbreak, which has been contained pending resolution' or 'Network services in the Midlands will be restored by 5 pm today';
- not providing such a long and tortuous series of interactive voice response (IVR) dialogues that people dialling in give up before connecting to the help service they were trying to access;
- asking whether the advice has resolved the issue and, if not, continuing the call until it has resolved the issue in order to avoid a repeat call from the same customer;
- knowing the range of things that can go wrong and having access to a knowledge base of tried and tested solutions;
- being able to invoke more technical support during the duration of a helpdesk call should the problem require further assistance;
- providing an excellent online self-service capability.

What is important is that the helpdesk becomes exactly that – a service that exists to help the customer rather than being simply a device for processing the customer's calls. Many companies regard helpdesks as a necessity but not a value-adding part of the IT organization, which is a shame because a good helpdesk will add much to both the perception of service quality and the reality of service delivery, which is important for any service-oriented organization. Few helpdesk staff are trained in how to deal with particularly bad users and then fail the organization if the user rings off or threatens to escalate the issue, which is not what a helpdesk is about.

The definition of a customer is different from that of a service user, however, as customers usually have some degree of influence on the service they receive. Customers are people who have specified a particular service, and that service will be more individual and less generic to the customers – they will feel a stronger sense of ownership and have an expectation of service quality set accordingly. Placing a customer in a call queue alongside thousands of service users is not good practice, and ITIL certainly does not require this, despite the efforts of many helpdesk vendors and IT staff alike, who regard the telephone as the only valid means of making contact with the IT function. Effective service provision for customers as defined here can come about through a number of means over and above those available to service users:

- providing different telephone numbers that place customers' calls higher up a telephone call queue or that route to a different facility;
- providing a named support person and individual contact details

- offering a 'walk-up' facility; this is frequently seen as the most effective way of providing service because customers like being able to talk to someone in person; it does not conflict with the practices described by ITIL incident management processes – they state clearly that every incident should be logged, not that contact has to be by telephone;
- providing post-contact follow-through and exploration of new service offerings.

It is important that, regardless of the service being offered, there is a clear distinction between a service user and a customer. IT has a responsibility to both groups and can make a difference to its own reputation as well as the capability of the group of clients that each of the service types represents.

TURNING CUSTOMERS INTO GOOD CUSTOMERS

It is important that all clients of IT service delivery interact with the organization in the most effective way possible. IT has a role to play in this interaction, and this can be evidenced on a number of levels:

- training;
- upskilling;
- business service management.

The explanation of the maturity stages in the Service Accession Model described in Chapters 1 and 2 showed that a key characteristic of the ultimate stage was that IT will ensure that customers derive best value from technology. This can be achieved in a number of ways, starting with basic training and then working up through skills acquisition and, finally, business service management in order to deliver world-class delivery standards. Taking each of these ways in turn, we will examine the key characteristics of each.

Training

It never fails to take people by surprise that new technology or a new application necessitates that people be trained in how to use it properly. This is sometimes done, most often by large, well-funded projects that can carry the cost of training customers as part of their authorized budget – but rarely beyond that stage. Even a well-funded project will miss the most obvious part of the training need, since budget ceases on implementation, and yet the simple aspects of staff turnover, business growth or relocation will dilute the ability of people to use the technology properly. Take as an example a new system that provides a call-centre application to an insurance company. This system is based on state-of-the-art telephony, integrated call scripting and sophisticated message-routing capabilities and will be operated by clerks with between two and three years of customer experience. Let us assume that there are 100 of these clerks and that all of them will be trained in the use of the application from the outset. The system goes live and the initial objectives are met – but does this mean the service is as good as it could be? This is doubtful because even the best training in the world does not cover all the likely service scenarios – the armed forces' maxim that 'no plan survives contact with the enemy' may not be entirely appropriate here but conveys the sense of what this issue concerns. It takes time for staff to be able to use a new service properly, much the same as it does to be able to drive a car properly. Passing a driving test is not the same as becoming a competent driver, since it takes experience and extra training to be able to cope with particular driving situations. The training required for customer clerks in this example to be able to absorb the range of technology, service options and customer care objectives cannot be covered by a generic 'sheep-dip' process. Figure 6.1 gives an example of how a staged approach to learning is often necessary.

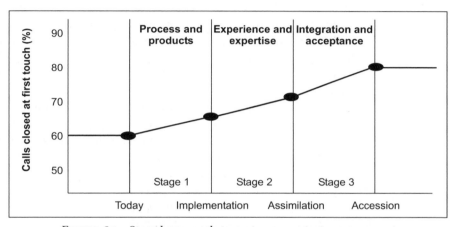

FIGURE 6.1 *Staged approach to customer contact management*

Training in customer care for an IT support function is frequently underestimated and, as Figure 6.1 shows, there are three stages involved in skilling the customer clerks – with around two days involved at each. Best practice in this regard will allocate as many as five days' initial training and two days' update training per employee each year, which is a high price but represents the cost of doing good business rather than paying it lip service. A simple way to regard the provision of training is to imagine that you are the person who will be facing the customer using this array of advanced technology options. How would you feel if you went to work each day knowing that you were aware of how to operate only a small portion of the functionality of the system?

IT professionals often operate on the basis that training is a cost and not a necessity and then skimp on training accordingly, which, if it was treated as a driving test, would mean our staff would not be allowed out on the road. It is important that we regard training in the effective use of IT as a means of improving roadworthiness, and we will explore the related concept of MOT (moment of truth) later in this chapter.

Training is also an issue when it is funded by an implementation project. Projects have a defined finish point and are then wound up, whereas service continues for years thereafter – despite relocation, turnover and attrition. A call-centre environment may experience as much as 25 per cent turnover each year, which means that after four years all our 100 (initially) trained staff will be new – and if the project finished four years ago, this raises the question as to how any new staff get the same level of capability awareness with which their predecessors were provided. The answer, of course, has to be that such turnover was anticipated and built into the ongoing IT training budget. If it is not, then the inevitable consequence is that new staff will operate the application at a lower level of capability than it was designed to deliver and thus negate much of the claimed business case benefit. This progressive degradation in value often leads to a reinvestment in applications development because it is believed – erroneously – that the problem needs solving by building a new solution, whereas the opposite is true. In the same way that advanced driving courses and refresher training exist to help car drivers get the most from their vehicles, so IT systems operation should be no different. Figure 6.2 illustrates the principle of progressive decline, which is characterized by a lack of strategic vision for IT services leading to an eventual – and almost always unnecessary – reinvestment through a lack of vision about how to keep the service offering running as it was designed. Once maximum value has been achieved from a new service, it is cheaper to maintain it than to replace it all from scratch.

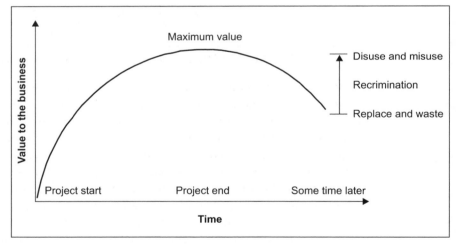

FIGURE 6.2   *Progressive decline of IT investment value*

So how can the training proposition as described in the Service Accession Model best be articulated? There are a number of ways, as described here.

Basic skills training

IT work today involves significant amounts of keyboard work, and yet few people are ever trained in how to touch-type. Secretaries and typing pools used to pride themselves on their ability to produce quality documents in short timescales based on achieving defined standards of competence in RSA keyboard skills, and yet this is assumed to be available to every new employee without the benefit of formal training. Tom Peters, a famous management expert, once said that there were only three attributes needed by a future business leader, and the first of these was being able to type. He was more right than he knew at the time, because his statement preceded the rapid decline of the formally trained secretary and an upsurge in the ubiquitous computer keyboard. Although IT is taught in schools as a formal part of the curriculum, few people are ever taught how to get the most out of the computer keyboard and the proportion of the population who can touch-type is low. Touch-typing involves typing using feel rather than sight and is sometimes taught by placing a membrane over the keys to prevent the learner from looking at what should come next. This method has been in use since the late nineteenth century, although many people still prefer to look at the keyboard while typing – and yet acquiring touch-typing skills could significantly increase productivity in the use of IT applications and document processing. If nothing else, staff should be encouraged to adopt formal training in order to increase the speed at which they can use a keyboard properly and there is a role for the IT training department to facilitate such training as the typing pool ceased to exist many years ago.

Applications training – ECDL

User competency improvement can be achieved by ensuring that every member of staff is brought up to the standard required to work on advanced PC-based systems. An effective way of achieving this aim is by use of the European Computer Driving Licence (ECDL), which is rapidly gaining acceptance as the most widely used method of achieving competency improvement in the UK and 107 other countries. ECDL is represented in the UK through the British Computer Society (BCS) and now has well over 1,000,000 users, with strategic adoption by a number of companies.

Examples of the key ECDL benefits from different sectors are shown below:

- NHS users have reported 38 minutes of extra time per day is available to spend with patients as a result of not struggling with PC issues and unfamiliarity.
- The Bank of England achieved a 50 per cent reduction in user IT support time.
- The London Borough of Islington reported 65 per cent more efficient use of IT in the team.
- Skanska improved worker productivity by 1.25 hours a week.

Some calculations have been provided to quantify what the organizational benefits might look like should ECDL be adopted. It has been assumed for the sake of these examples that a company's per-user costs are £23.40 per hour, and the tables reproduced in this chapter are based on two figures – a conservative view that more effective use of the IT service will save 30 minutes a week and a pragmatic view based on an estimate of the service downtime as reported through the helpdesk systems for typical companies that shows a possible 7.2 per cent productivity loss as a result of poor training. In reality, lost user productivity will lie somewhere between these examples but is still large. The rationale behind using both 30 minutes and 7.2 per cent is an important one. The work the author has done in recent years has shown that users in a corporate environment consistently lose an average of 7.2 per cent of their working week through not using their IT facilities to the maximum extent possible. If this was addressed through a formal structured training programme, then those users would be more productive and their time could be used for other purposes, such as product sales and marketing, or could lead to the same work being done by fewer people – sometimes a relevant option. ECDL is unlikely to be able to address every possible user skill issue because these may be affected by the business processes being used or the need for specific application knowledge, and so 30 minutes has been chosen to represent 20 per cent of the 7.2 per cent overall user productivity gap – which is 2.5 hours a week in total – that ECDL could realistically address; this is shown in Table 6.1. We will look at a technique that can help to address the remaining 80 per cent in the next section of this chapter.

TABLE 6.1   *Organizational value statement from gaining 30 minutes per week*

Assume your users gain 30 minutes per person per week			
Average hours gained per person per week			0.50
Total hours gained			230,000
Working weeks gained			6133
Total number of computers/ employees in your organization	Overheads per hour (weighted average salary)	Working weeks in a year	Annual productivity value gained
10,000	£23.40	46	£5,382,000

The benefits shown are expressed in terms of an annual productivity value gained, which is felt to be an effective way of quantifying the purpose of training, although other measures could also be used. As a means of gaining attention, however, this measure is capable of being used in any enterprise.

ECDL can be developed and delivered in-house, on external premises or at a college, as appropriate. Most commercial organizations can achieve certification to deliver training in-house, and this route is financially viable, as the following case studies illustrate. Any initial training, including 'train the trainer', can be done in conjunction with specialist third-party providers.

CASE STUDY 1 – TELECOMMUNICATIONS SERVICE PROVIDER

Benefits – reduction in utilization of the IT helpdesk	60%
Cost of training, assessment and user documentation	£56 per user
Time commitment from learners to ECDL programme	1 hour per week
Training resource level needed in IT	1 person
Facilities needed	Learning centre, PC workstations, ECDL software

Start-up costs were low, consisting mainly of the cost of employing an IT learning manager, a £300 accreditation fee for an in-house centre and the capital cost of providing a small number of dedicated PCs – which could have been redeployed PCs. The project met its objectives of reducing helpdesk traffic by 60 per cent, which recovered significantly more benefit than the cost as the helpdesk was outsourced and so the client paid on a per-call basis.

As described here, implementing a formal, outcome-based learning scheme such as ECDL has a small administration overhead and cost of delivery, since course material has already been developed and can be used at low incremental cost.

CASE STUDY 2 – THE NATIONAL HEALTH SERVICE

The NHS adopted ECDL as a method of skilling its staff in the use of computer technology some years ago and is continuing to use it. A recently reported example of the use of ECDL in the NHS is known as Wave 19, which covered a wide range of front-line medical staff, as opposed to purely back-office personnel, with all results based on formal customer surveys. Of the 262 medical personnel surveyed, 61 per cent were positive that they could do their jobs better as a result of undertaking the course, with 15 per cent believing they could save up to an hour a day as a result of being able to use the software better than they could before being trained. As 30 per cent of the respondents were general practiioners (GPs), clinicians and staff in the nursing, health visiting and other professions allied to medicine, such as ambulance staff, this benefit can be interpreted directly into an improvement in the provision of primary care. One-third of the staff that received training were in the age range 45–54 years, indicating that it is not only junior staff who should be targeted for computer training. Satisfaction in the way ECDL had been implemented in the NHS study was nearly 85 per cent, and 95 per cent of all candidates said they would recommend the training programme to their colleagues – in effect, allowing staff rather than the trainers to be the best advocates of computer training.

Upskilling – INVEST

Realizing the claimed benefit from the level of investment represented by strategic developments such as enterprise resource planning (ERP) and sophisticated customer information systems (CIS) means that staff must know how to use them properly. Despite this seeming an obvious statement, it is rarely the case that 100 per cent of the users of such systems have 100 per cent of the knowledge to do their jobs properly 100 per cent of the time, and this acts as a limitation on organizational capability. The skills shortfall is something in which IT can play a major role, and addressing and upskilling IT-enabled workers to function in the most efficient manner possible is a core component of the world-class service delivery proposition. This can be done either as part of an ERP or CIS implementation programme or separately, because the processes involved depend not on the technology being installed but on the differences between required and actual skills. This difference has been assessed through call closure analyses of helpdesk traffic as a loss of 7.2 per cent of the effective working week. Table 6.2 describes the potential productivity quantification that suboptimal skills represents.

TABLE 6.2 *Organizational value statement from improving productivity by 7.2%*

Assume your users gain 7.2% productivity per person per week			
Average hours gained per person per week			2.52
Total hours gained			1,159,200
Working weeks gained			30,912
Total number of computers/ employees in your organization	Overheads per hour (weighted average salary)	Working weeks in a year	Annual productivity value gained
10000	£23.40	46	£27,125,280

One methodology that is designed specifically to address this difference is INVEST, which is a combination of a business process, a methodology and a toolset that provides the technology to manage both the process and the customers. INVEST was originally a product of Moebius (UK) Ltd, a specialist training company, although it has now been adopted by the Capita Group plc, which is able to provide opportunities for a greater degree of adoption than was previously possible.

INVEST was devised in the 1990s in response to a requirement to gain more productivity from workstation-equipped users in a high-street bank, which defined a target for user-competency improvement. This target was designed to focus both the IT function and the business departments on the need to show a demonstrable improvement in productivity as a result of the level of investment in new systems. An aspirational target of 20 per cent per annum skill improvement was proposed to act as a focus for the scale of training intervention required, which was clearly non-incremental. The emphasis was not only about training people in shrink-wrapped office productivity applications, for which approaches such as ECDL could have been offered, but also about developing an integrated business process designed to ensure that everyone had all the skills they needed in order to do their jobs all of the time. It was recognized that delivering this scale of quantified improvement was outside the scope of a conventional IT training scheme, and so a new methodology was created. The supporting technology and assessment frameworks have been progressively extended to the point where the methodology can now be either run in-house or offered on an externally hosted basis as appropriate.

The methodology used by INVEST:

- identifies the business skills required within a department;
- identifies the current skills of the individuals within that department;
- identifies any additional skills required on a individual basis;
- designs a learning plan for each individual;
- identifies the most appropriate delivery method;
- delivers the additional skills required;
- assesses an individual's progress on an ongoing basis.

Courseware is designed and developed based on the identified need – this could be a standard software package or a unique internal system, the difference in the training being that it is geared specifically to the way in which business departments use their IT systems.

The methodology allows IT to 'measure' skill at defined points in the process and the productivity improvement target is dependent on the capability of staff as discovered at the start of the process. However, business departments using this methodology have experienced between 15 and 45 per cent productivity gain from their people, who ended up being far more confident and able to handle the complex workflows presented by modern systems. This productivity gain can be reinvested for business benefit, either in terms of handling more work with the same number of staff or by reducing staff numbers to match current work levels. The overall result was extremely positive, since business departments fund the training intervention required as they can see exactly what level of benefit they gained from it. An IT training department can therefore be responsible for initiating and managing the process, doing both the initial and ongoing skill assessment and managing the INVEST application and toolset.

Recent developments have enabled INVEST to access the skills profiles defined by SFIA and PRINCE 2, providing a bridge between the methodology and current best-practice IT management frameworks. An example of how

INVEST has been used in the public sector is described in the case study below.

CASE STUDY – SERVICE BIRMINGHAM LTD.

Service Birmingham is a strategic partnership between Birmingham City Council and Capita that will support the IT transformation of the way in which the council works, in order to improve services and contribute to its efficiency agenda.

The development of people within Service Birmingham is at the core of the plans. The first stage of this was to use the INVEST methodology to develop a process for capturing the current skill sets of the staff within Service Birmingham, and the Skills Framework for the Information Age (SFIA) was chosen as the assessment framework. The data captured from the assessment process were stored within the INVEST database and the skills requirements for each role were identified by assessing jobs on the same basis.

This means Service Birmingham now has the ability to use these data for development planning, risk assessment, resource management – a whole range of applications. Fundamentally, it enables the organization to construct an individual development plan based around each individual's core objectives.

As the process is generic, it can be adapted to cater for any type of training intervention and, if used regularly, will ensure that staff turnover and new skills requirements are taken into account. Figure 6.3 shows a summary of the INVEST methodology, which includes feedback about how well the new skills have been acquired in order to repopulate individual skill profiles.

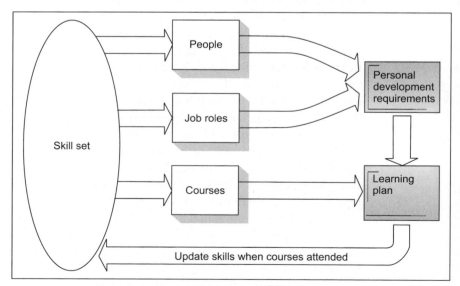

FIGURE 6.3 *Summary of the INVEST methodology*

In order to illustrate this methodology in action, the screen shot in Figure 6.4 is provided to show an example of how required skills are matched against current skills in order to define a suitable training plan for that individual. This example is for an SFIA skill, but the approach is universal.

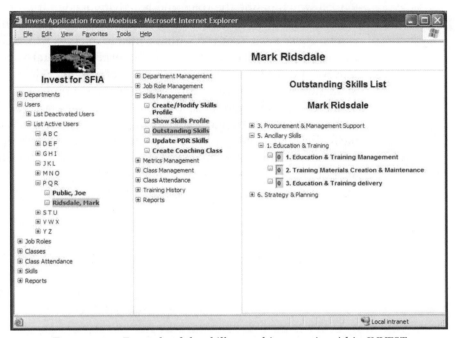

FIGURE 6.4   *Example of the skills-matching matrix within INVEST*

The ultimate aim of using techniques such as INVEST and ECDL is to align the skills of the people who use your service to the capabilities of the technology for which the business has paid a lot of money. This is the essence of service management, and a department with an ambition to accede to world-class status needs to develop a training delivery strategy.

BUSINESS SERVICE LEVEL MANAGEMENT

We examined the issue of SLAs in Chapter 3 and reported that their attainment was becoming increasingly irrelevant to the user. Despite this, however, the SLA is still regarded by the majority of service delivery organizations as being an indispensable part of their operational toolkit. It is true that SLAs are still required and act as a form of health check for contract reviews as well as forming part of the operational design specification for a new systems delivery project. The SLA is not a high-level process defined by ITIL, however, which is why it needs to be seen in a wider context – service level management (SLM). The overall goal of an SLM approach is to maintain and improve service quality, which is why it is of intrinsically more value than an SLA, which usually defines only attainment targets rather than improvement actions and methods. SLM relies on SLAs to provide the underpinning mechanism by which service delivery targets are met, but this is basically all that SLAs should be used for. Of more value to the satisfaction of the design goals of SLM are a range of other processes such as operational level agreements (OLAs) which define the roles and reactivity needed from internal IT suppliers and contract targets in place with external and other third-party providers. These need a context within which to operate, which is best provided by means of a service catalogue listing everything that you do (and why) plus an approach to service improvement in order to discharge the goal of SLM. Although the classical approach to service improvement is often known as service improvement programme (SIP), the author advocates a different path to achieve the design goal for world-class SLM, which is to manage the business service and not just the mechanistic approach to operational service delivery. This hierarchy of service-level processes is shown in Figure 6.5, including the business service management layer.

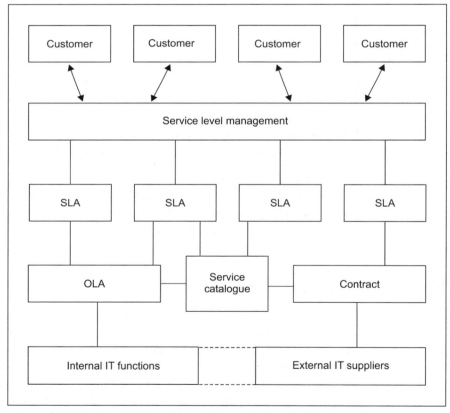

FIGURE 6.5 *Representation of the role of service level management*

The representation in Figure 6.5 is not the same as defined by ITIL because, unfortunately, customers do not behave in the way in which process designers would like them to. Instead, the representation allows the service delivery team to build a service from a defined set of component parts that are listed in a service catalogue and supported by underpinning contracts with external IT providers and OLAs, a form of internal contract, with the rest of IT and other departments such as premises, procurement and legal.

Based on the SLAs that are then drawn up, the service delivery team can manage the customer base by means of a service management approach that certainly uses SLAs but not as the primary rationale for the relationship. This point is important because customer behaviour is influenced heavily by the way in which information is presented to customers, and effective SLM can play a big part in creating a positive relationship. There are a number of reasons for this:

- If the customer is a consumer, no SLA will exist in the first place.
- No customer, whether internal or external, is likely to sign an SLA for a generic shared service such as email, telephony or web services.
- Even if a signed SLA is in force, service delivery will not be able to defend downtime caused by a loss of service – even if within the SLA – if it happened at an inconvenient time to the customer or if it affected a key opinion former.
- Customers will focus on the difference between their expectations of service quality – 100 per cent – with the SLA report, which may show a lower figure. Providing detailed SLA figures is actually giving your customer an opportunity to criticize, which is what people like doing.
- Customers will also ignore any volume or time-of-day variations in their utilization of service, even if the SLA specifies such parameters.

So, the SLA is not the best vehicle to represent service quality, and customers' opinions will be influenced by how service is reported to them, which is why business service management is a more significant component of SLM than is the SLA. As an example of this, effective SLM will report on business-activity levels that IT has been able to satisfy – such as how many loans were opened in the month, how many billing queries were satisfied and how many customer statements were sent out. When service managers go to meetings with service reports based on showing how their customer KPIs have been met, it is interesting to see how few of them bother to ask about that server outage or email glitch. This way of taking responsibility for the achievement of customer outcomes will significantly influence the way in which service is perceived and place responsibility for application and infrastructure management at the level at which it belongs, with the underlying providers. Although this is properly in the domain of SLM, it can be referred to under other names, such as a business impact agreement, in order to differentiate it from the conventional SLM approach described through ITIL.

Used properly, this type of business-focused SLM approach will help to get service delivery represented more appropriately on the management teams of a corporate entity because the customer will perceive a greater level of interest, knowledge and understanding of key business outcomes. This has a different manifestation in the servicing of consumers, who do not have a conventional representation within IT anyway, except perhaps through user groups, forums and bulletin boards. A similar approach can be taken to consumer service delivery by reporting on how many orders a web service has handled, or how many new customers were added rather than what the server availability was like last month, which most people don't want to know unless they are looking for a means to criticize you.

Criticism may well be justified even when SLM is being managed properly because something will always go wrong – this is not a perfect world. If a business target is breached because of an IT problem, then this is worse than if an SLA is breached, because the business outcome is what pays the bills for IT. So part of an effective SLM strategy is based around having a recovery plan that will allow your customer to regain the business loss as a consequence of service outage. We explained in Chapter 5 that service will be judged more highly if something goes wrong but is then recovered in a way that exceeds normal customer expectations, compared with when service is delivered normally. Again, this is a perceptual issue that SLM can address, but the SLA cannot, and gives rise to the concept of having a recovery strategy. A recovery strategy can be likened to the service that a retailer may offer to replace or refund an item that is no longer wanted. If a customer buys, say, an item of clothing that doesn't fit, the retailer (through an unwritten SLA) is entirely within its rights to decline to exchange the article. However, best practice in retailing is to keep customer attention and therefore most good stores will exchange or offer a refund for unwanted articles. A similar story can be told in respect of IT where a loss of business capability caused by a cessation in IT capability can be recovered without long-term damage to the relationship, and this is covered in the next section.

USING THE MOT PRINCIPLE FOR IT SERVICES

Moments of truth (MOTs) happen every time a customer comes into contact with your organization. In a transport system, this might be as short as 15 seconds per encounter between a customer and an employee, but this is still long enough for an opinion to be formed about the company that the employee represents. MOTs happen all the time, and customers form either conscious or subconscious impressions of how a company operates by how each individual aspect of service is delivered. What happens as a result of cumulative MOTs is that customers make long-term decisions about who they wish to do business with based on what is often a remarkably short service exposure. The MOT concept was first postulated by Scandinavian Airlines in the 1980s as a means of restoring the company to good health by removing everything that was not adding value to the customer experience. It was calculated that every one of their 10 million customers came into contact with 5 employees for 15 seconds each, an annual customer exposure of some 208,000 hours. In that time, those 50 million MOTs did not consider how well the aircraft might have been maintained, what level of capital investment the company was planning for the coming year or how well the stores administration worked. Instead, those 208,000 hours of contact were spent assessing the quality of the 'contract' between the airline and the passenger, including how smart the staff appeared – and yet these issues were not discussed at board meetings, whereas the items mentioned earlier were. The quality of a customer contract is therefore based on the quality of customer contact, and this is ideally suited for consideration within an IT service delivery department because the underlying issues are the same – both an airline and an IT delivery organization exist to provide customer service.

Customer contact in IT

A typical corporate organization may receive 15,000 service calls through its helpdesks a month; whether they are internal or external calls doesn't matter in this context. Fieldwork undertaken by the author in recent years reveals that three employees are typically involved in each service request for an average of 6 minutes and 35 seconds on each occasion, a total of 59,250 hours of contact time each year. This level of exposure is clearly far greater than the amount of time IT functions believe they are exposed to customers – which may be a simple calculation based on, say, 10 managers attending a monthly customer meeting for two hours at a time, a total of 240 hours a year. It often comes as quite a surprise when a corporate decision is announced that, for instance, the IT department is being considered as a potential for being outsourced or that service quality is not – to the customer – what the IT management team understands it to be. The inputs to such decisions arise not from experiencing 'service as normal' or the 240 hours a year of what may well have been effective management contribution, but the cumulative exposure to 59,250 hours a year of service experience, which is why the MOT concept is an important one for service delivery to embrace.

Customer contact with IT transcends the SLA and the effectiveness of the technology provided, since it is based on perceptions and personal experiences. An anecdotal example taken from an annual customer survey revealed that a branch manager's opinion of the hardware maintenance company being used to support her cashiers' equipment was based solely around the personal hygiene of the engineer rather than his ability to do the job. This type of feedback is common and yet is rarely sought; if it is sought, it is rarely acted upon, despite the fact that such issues can be addressed more readily, if more sensitively, than something of a systemic nature. Systemic issues fall into two main categories – service experience and personal exposure – and we will look at both of these aspects in turn.

The service experience

CASE STUDY 1 – AN OFFICE BLOCK

At 12.45 am on Boxing Day, the cold-water tanks in the roof of a three-storey office block froze because they hadn't been used for some time and weren't lagged well enough to protect them from an especially cold snap. This ruptured the tank walls and dumped not only the entire contents of the tanks (about 2000 gallons) but also the consequential inrush of water from the mains supply into the building. Because of the time of day, this was not detected for some time; when it was eventually discovered by the night watch, the water had brought down the ceilings on two floors and had covered the ground floor to a depth of several inches. As well as rendering the electricity supply unsafe, the deluge had also soaked 2000 user workstations and several server rooms, rendering the company unable to do business. The IT business continuity procedure was invoked and resulted in a restoration activity that repaired, replaced or isolated the equipment such that when the company was due to open for business again, on 28 December, it could do so without a noticeable effect on its customers. This involved the IT team spending their Christmas holiday on unplanned and difficult work with minimal supplier support, and yet it was very well received, with accolades all around from the top management, particularly for the support staff who arrived on site within an hour of being called out, complete with mops. This moment of truth was one with which the IT team rightly deserved to be credited.

CASE STUDY 2 – A CASH MACHINE NETWORK

A large financial institution had upgraded the software on its cash machine (ATM) network some months earlier. At one second past midnight on 1st September, the whole network shut down, rendering every machine inoperable. Worse still, because the system was also used to authorize cash transactions over branch counters and internet banking transactions, customers could not access their accounts. Action wasn't taken until the next day because the operators did not read the error logs. Unfortunately, the next day was a Saturday and every branch in every town opened for business without the ability to dispense cash through the ATMs or over the counter. Not surprisingly, customer reaction varied from disappointment, through incredulity to outright abuse and, as the fault persisted for several days, branch staff had to cope with a very adverse public reaction, which affected many of the staff, such that they either resigned or went on sick leave. The IT response 'We're working on it' did not stand scrutiny for long. After the fault was eventually found to be a programming logic error, which meant no month number higher than 8 was deemed by the system to be valid, it was said that IT had failed in its duty to manage such incidents properly.

The interesting thing to note about these two case studies is that neither of them was actually caused by service delivery – in the first case it was a plumbing problem, and in the second it was a systems error. However, neither the plumbers nor the programmers were responsible for managing the service users, but in one case this was done very well and in the second it was done very badly. Different organizations manage exposure between their services staff and the customer base in different ways, and yet the MOT effect is the same – customers want to know that when things go badly wrong, the response is immediate, visible, well-communicated and business-focused. In both cases, the incidents took place out of normal office hours and so the management response could not be conventional, although in case study 1 it was effective whereas in case study 2 it was not. Service delivery is not an office-hours activity because when this type of customer experience is involved management needs to both act and be seen to act.

The personal experience

Another aspect of MOT is that of forming opinion. Returning to the example of a branch manager judging maintenance quality based on an engineer's personal hygiene, we can see that who we are matters to the customer. This can be evidenced by the words we use and the way we say them as well as by what we wear and how often we shower, and it is important to look at the language examples that typically mar good customer service experiences. Real examples such as those shown below are commonplace:

'It's not been designed like that, so use it in a different (unspecified) way. '

'It doesn't work because you don't know how to use it properly. '

'Don't complain to me – I'm not in charge. '

'I can't do that – the system won't let me. '

Take for example a supermarket on a Friday evening. Every checkout is busy and the cashier on one lane finds an item without a barcode on it and so cannot continue scanning the customer's goods. The whole lane is therefore stopped until a supervisor can be called to intervene, which may involve going to the shelves and finding an identical item that does have a barcode on it. In the meantime, both the customer directly affected as well as the rest of the people in the queue are getting very frustrated, as is the cashier, who is in the limelight for the wrong reasons. This is not empowerment but an example of a process that has gone wrong. MOT demands service empowerment if it is to achieve a benefit in terms of the customer experience, in this example by the supermarket allowing cashiers to look up the price of an item themselves on a database or – if necessary – by giving the customer the item free of charge or at a nominal charge. It is easy to understand the positive impression this gives the customer as well as how the cashier might feel about the job by being granted more freedom to act in terms of customer service. It would be easy to criticize this example by saying that it gives licence to either the customer or the cashier to act dishonestly, which may be true – but when both methods have been experienced, there is a very clear view from both sides of the transaction as to which method is more effective. The issue of empowerment and how this can be applied in a typical hierarchical organization is shown diagrammatically in Figure 6.6.

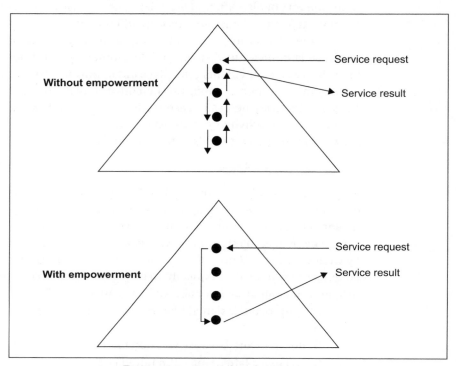

FIGURE 6.6   *Examples of empowerment*

The example of a supermarket cashier is not the only way in which staff can be empowered to deliver service. As can be seen from the pyramids in Figure 6.6, staff at one level often receive requests for service that are passed on to people more able to deal with them. This need not be the same person of whom the request is made, providing that whomever is delegated the task is capable of performing it properly, *including the customer experience*. This requires that every member of staff, regardless of function, be aware of what a good customer experience feels like and be able to project it accordingly. It is an issue that not every member of staff will feel that they need to be trained in customer service, especially in the deeper technical disciplines, or that they don't have time to deal with customer issues. This is a good manifestation of the attitude that needs to be overcome, because third-line technical support roles are frequently part of the 59,250 contact hours a year exposed earlier in this section and can often contribute much of the negative customer reaction. It is accepted that systems programmers need not come to work in suits or that installation engineers do not have to attend elocution lessons before being allowed near a customer, but equally it must be accepted that what is said and how it is said will create an impression. Table 6.3 provides examples of negative language in the left-hand column and a better version in the right-hand column.

TABLE 6.3   *The new language of service experience*

Old language	MOT language
We'll have to rebuild the server	We built the server properly the first time it was installed
We can't do that – we're too busy	We can do what you want by an agreed date, which will be . . .
We can't do that because . . .	We'll gladly do it, providing that . . .
We don't have the budget for that	Let's work on a new funding request
Customers are asking us for too much	We work on the value of your custom
This doesn't meet our standards	We will create a new standard for this because it's a great idea
We are constrained by IT head count	We are part of a global IT economy and therefore can find as many skilled resources as are needed
But it worked OK last week!	We have a zero tolerance for defects
Look at it from the IS viewpoint	Look at it from a customer viewpoint
I need you to know that I'm good	I need to demonstrate that I'm good
What's the priority of this work?	What's the payback of this work?

The phrases in Table 6.3 are all taken from real-life observations of IT departments struggling with the concept of excellent customer experiences. This issue, although not devised by a standards committee, has been recognized even in service delivery terms; ISO/IEC 20000, which became effective in December 2005, lists both customer satisfaction and people satisfaction as an overall part of its effective operation. MOT is one of the powerful techniques that can be used to change the culture of a service delivery department by changing the attitudes of the people that work within it, and it can be put into effect with relatively little management overhead. For an MOT programme to work successfully, the following components must be taken into consideration:

- management sponsorship;
- customer awareness of the programme and input to it in terms of why customers believe IT is providing a poor service experience;
- development of common customer objectives and standards;
- establishment of (at least) one direct customer service objective for each member of IT, including third-line and operational resources;
- commitment to address non-compliance with MOT objectives.

The cost of this type of exercise equates to about 10 days management time to establish the ground rules and about two days per member of staff per year to set the objectives and put them into practice with customers. This time allocation is relatively low because each transaction lasts just over six minutes, and so it is the planning and training that takes the time when devising an MOT programme, not the doing. Having seen evidence of this approach deployed in several organizations, the author is convinced of its merits.

SUMMARY

- Understand who is a user and who is a customer and treat them accordingly.
- Develop good user IT skills as part of a value-adding service proposition.
- Employ service level management (SLM) rather than service level agreements (SLAs) in order to manage customer expectations and to raise the quality of dialogue with people at the receiving end of your delivery.
- Empower staff at all levels to be able to satisfy customer needs.
- Adopt a moment of truth (MOT) strategy to deliver a consistent and well-perceived quality of service, including perceptual and personal issues.

7 Governing service delivery

The current wave of new regulations including the Companies Act, the more widely reported Sarbanes–Oxley Act and initiatives such as Basel II and International Financial Reporting Standards (IFRS) have inevitably had a large impact on the way in which IT decisions and controls are implemented, as indeed did earlier legislation such as the Distance Selling Regulations and the Data Protection Act in the UK. There is no single industry definition of 'governance' and hence the expression has become widely interpreted to represent authoritarianism or as something that has a negative connotation. This negativity is reinforced once the term 'compliance' is used in conjunction with 'governance' as a means of reinforcing the 'police officer' aspect to corporate management focus. However, governance is, simply, the way in which control over any particular function is achieved, and it is a natural part of leadership and policy setting, which are the more obvious components of overall IT management responsibility.

This chapter sets out the scope and way in which an IT organization can demonstrate effective self-governance at the same time as retaining the leadership role for service delivery and achievement of an outstanding customer experience, against the backdrop of a wide range of compliance, control and corporate reporting requirements. Governance in some IT organizations is managed by a department separate from service delivery, although, as the attributes of control and reporting are shared between them, this is arguably not the best way to approach the subject. The case is set out here for governance to be managed as an integral part of the world-class service department and not as a clerical addition to it, and the scope of governance as considered in this chapter includes a number of topics that are significant in the overall management framework for IT so they have been represented here as different aspects of the same overall regime.

DEFINITION AND FRAMEWORKS

Although there is no single standard IT industry definition of governance, there are a number of relevant interpretations. One leading interpretation has been defined by the Office of Government Commerce (OGC), which explains that governance is concerned with *accountability* and *responsibility* in terms of the standards that are used to direct and control an IT department. These standards involve both the IT function and the wider organization that is the customer of IT, driven by the realization that an ever increasing proportion of services will be delivered electronically and in real time. The OGC goes on to specify that governance must concern itself particularly with organizational issues, such as how priorities and partnerships are managed; with management issues, such as how roles and responsibilities are established to manage business change and operational services; and with policy issues, such as what frameworks and boundaries are established for decision making. The OGC is, of course, also the author of ITIL and an enthusiastic supporter of ISO/IEC 20000, which makes it uniquely able to specify IT control prerequisites in the UK. At the time of writing, ITIL is undergoing a major refresh – sometimes known as ITIL v3 – to reflect the increasing shift from basic operational processes to the entire service lifecycle. The scope of ISO/IEC 20000, which is largely based on ITIL, has been explored in Chapter 4 and is reproduced again in Figure 7.1 to show the disciplines of service reporting, security management and the two major relationship processes that will increasingly be used to discharge corporate demands for transparency of control over IT.

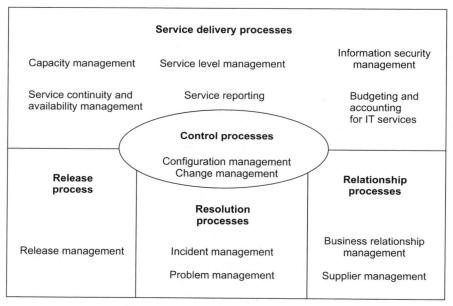

FIGURE 7.1   *ISO/IEC 20000 schematic*

Another leading interpretation of governance comes from the USA-led IT Governance Institute (ITGI), which helps to define standards and tools to ensure that IT supports business goals as well as appropriately managing risks and opportunities in the business exploitation of IT. The ITGI also offers a standard governance tool – Control Objectives for Information Technology (CobiT) – which has been in existence since 1996. It is positioned as a practical toolkit for IT governance because following both earlier and current control demands, corporate governance and risk management have become increasingly important issues to businesses. CobiT is structured around the whole IT lifecycle, and Sarbanes–Oxley requirements can be satisfied using it. This is more of a compliance initiative than one of governance and so is not debated here, although it is necessary to distinguish between them.

The context for governance

Most companies with business interests in the USA have heard of the Sarbanes–Oxley Act and, to a lesser extent, the comparable 2004 UK legislation known as the Companies (Audit, Investigations and Community Enterprise) Act, which have both arisen as a result of reported corporate failures such as Enron and WorldCom. The Acts are worded differently but mean the same thing in that companies at corporate level have strict obligations in relation to the management and reporting of financial transactions, including the details of the accuracy of that financial information. Of course, it can be argued that an effective enterprise accounting system such as Oracle Financials or mySAP ERP already satisfies this, but where Section 404 of Sarbanes–Oxley and the equivalent obligations in the amended Companies Act differ from established practice is that the information provided to, or accessed by, auditors has to be certified by *corporate management* as being accurate.

Both Oracle and mySAP will report on the quality of data contained within the scope of their deployment, but this may not be enough on its own to satisfy the new accuracy criteria. For instance, have data been accessed only by the relevant people, and does an audit trail exist of any changes that might have been made? How certain can a company be that privileged access controls needed by IT have not been used to circumvent system controls and manipulate underlying data? These have always been legitimate concerns, but the audit rules allow much greater scope for questions and probing, with regulators likely to become increasingly outspoken on company transparency and accountability. Audit firms will also look to ensure that the quality of data and processes that manipulate data are as good as they need to be in order to protect themselves against the potential for accusations of sloppy work, as they have been heavily criticized in relation to corporate misdoings in Europe and the USA.

Again, these issues have always had to be managed and reported, and diligent companies have been certifying data quality for many years. Such reporting requirements may be seen only as negative controls rather than enabling controls over IT activity – which is rather unfair because, like driving a car, more than just brakes are needed to control its movement. But the bigger the engine, the bigger the brakes need to be, as well as the increasing skill of the driver and the complexity of regulations that govern the car's presence on the road. Depending on the application, the governance over driving on a public highway involves such rules as restrictions on driving hours, the use of tachographs and more demanding driving tests – which seems reasonable when you consider what the driver of a 44-tonne petrol tanker is responsible for when compared with the driver of an ordinary saloon car.

Use of balanced controls

What both ISO/IEC 20000 and CobiT offer is a balance in terms of how IT can be managed. The detail of both frameworks is similar in respect of the delivery and support of IS operations, with CobiT adding more audit and controls emphasis but ISO/IEC 20000 offering more scope to manage innovation. Making visible the achievements and accountabilities of an IS organization therefore leads to the need for a reporting mechanism to show progress against such factors as IT strategy, financial effectiveness, control status, operational delivery and customer satisfaction. This balance between strategy, control and performance – the driver, the brake and the throttle – is best achieved by the development of a dashboard, or scorecard, which looks at all these issues in an holistic way. After all, boards of directors are not only accountable for the effectiveness of audit controls but also have a responsibility to their shareholders for measures such as capital growth and dividends, with the annual report explaining how all these factors affect each other. So the development and use of a balanced scorecard, or dashboard, is an effective way for an IT function to show its capability to enable and control both simultaneously and transparently. Figure 7.2 shows how a twin-track scorecard will allow focus on both aspects of the control environment, that which manages risk and that which creates new value.

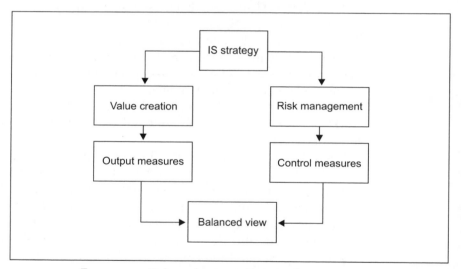

FIGURE 7.2 *Balanced scorecard approach to governance*

A balanced scorecard also needs to take account of the customer and the staff who work in the IS department, especially those at the front end. An holistic approach based on, for example, the EFQM Excellence Model as described in Chapter 4 will allow the focus to be referenced back to a repeatable standard rather than being merely a single company initiative. Finally, the state of control technology is such that a real-time reporting mechanism can be used to alert responsible management to actual or likely control breaches, based on ISO 17799 and ISO/IEC 20000 management criteria. ITIL control process monitoring is an effective way of ensuring sustainable ISO/IEC 20000 compliance and, hence, adherence to IS governance.

Figure 7.3 shows an example of how ITIL achievements may be reported on using automated data capture and integration with a balanced scorecard.

Highest negative performance

	Code	Name	Gap% ▲	Change %	Date
🔍	Capacity	Capacity management	−22.4%	−0.6% ↓	9/9/06
🔍	Change	Change management	−19.7%	12.9% ↑	9/9/06
🔍	Incident	Incident management	−0.2%	39.1% ↑	9/9/06

Highest positive performance

	Code	Name	Gap% ▲	Change %	Date
🔍	Release	Release management	22.9%	0.5% ↑	9/9/06
🔍	Service	Service level management	5.7%	12.4%	9/9/06
🔍	Continuity	Continuity management	3.6%	−7% ↓	9/9/06

FIGURE 7.3   *ITIL reporting dashboard*

What this type of automation allows is the direct linkage of the status of individual IT processes to the target set for them, and to be able to report any variance. This has been used effectively for KPI monitoring for some time but is now available for process quality monitoring as well. Given the additional features introduced by ISO/IEC 20000, with its enhanced focus on management controls and service delivery, such a dashboard is likely to offer one of the few cost-effective ways to demonstrate governance and for targets to be revised dynamically as priorities change.

Call to action

Compliance and governance are complementary initiatives – the new Companies Act, emerging standards and international legislation have all ensured that companies will have to focus on controls more than ever before. The good news is that solutions exist that can allow IT departments to manage their own governance in a transparent and effective way, and therefore keep the cost of regulatory compliance at an acceptable level. But this will be the case only if the way in which IT is managed takes account of the basics behind the requirements for greater reporting and accountability – namely, assurance to corporate management that there are no skeletons in the data centre and that audit certification can be signed without undue cause for concern.

This situation can be achieved if the following steps are taken:

- Understand all the governance requirements in your sector.
- Deploy a quality management framework incorporating ISO/IEC 20000.
- Develop and use a balanced scorecard to demonstrate that IS recognizes the need for both enabling and preventive measures.
- Be prepared to define and instrument all your key processes.
- Use the compliance and governance framework to demonstrate the value that service delivery brings to the business in enabling effective audit controls.

INFORMATION SECURITY MANAGEMENT AND THE ROLE OF STANDARDS

A complementary topic to governance is that of security management, since concerns about security have existed for as long as has humankind. This chapter explains how security management and service management are part of the same overall remit – to run an effective enterprise information architecture. As they are but different aspects of the same objective, it can be argued that security management can coexist with service delivery as they are both part of IT governance. Security is taken for granted until something goes wrong, when visibility goes through the roof and management starts to hunt for someone to blame. Although this is understandable, it can also be recognized quickly that exactly the same characteristic applies to service delivery. Information security is a topic that has its own terminology, standards and champions and is either given too much or not enough prominence, depending on who is involved. However, we use information more today than at any time in our collective past, and access to – and the accuracy of – that information is an assumed right. Information security is defined here, and then shown why not only is it relevant to the discipline of service delivery but also that it should be managed alongside it.

Definition of security

Information is an asset that, like any other business asset, has value to an organization and so needs protecting. Whether that information is in paper or electronic format doesn't matter in terms of the business safeguards needed, although the main interest level is clearly in the electronic format since this is what IT deals with everyday. Information security is defined here as representing the preservation of the following:

- *confidentiality:* ensuring that information is accessible only to those authorized to access it;
- *integrity:* safeguarding the accuracy and completeness of information and its processing;
- *availability:* ensuring that users can get access to information and any associated assets when required.

So, it isn't hard to understand the correlation between the objectives of information security management and what service managers should be doing every day. For instance, good security is achieved by implementing a set of controls, policies, practices and procedures along with organizational structures and software support. This is so like how formal service management disciplines are structured that information security management should become a natural extension to scope for a department acceding to world-class status. However, service credibility has to have been achieved already otherwise the justification to take on more responsibility is unlikely to exist.

Security controls and regulation

There are few formal controls governing service management in isolation, but there are many concerning security management. These actually determine what service controls should exist and to what level of compliance with rules, statutes, regulations and industry standards. There are several control regimes that govern security, with the most obvious one being ISO 17799 and the complementary standard ISO 27001. Although ISO 27001 defines an information security management system (ISMS), ISO 17799 details the individual security controls that may be selected and applied as part of the ISMS as well as establishing guidelines and general principles. ISO 17799 is the successor to BS 7799 Part 1 and details 127 controls in 10 focus areas – but, of course, not all of these are needed in every organization, and many of them are capable of interpretation. This is where care is needed because, unlike service management, security management can be overdone 'to be on the safe side' and organizations sometimes end up being burdened by the weight of control.

Although we would not want just anyone to be able to see our bank accounts, the protection needed over, say, our postcode may be much less important and so the controls need to be different. It is this aspect of security that confuses people most, because an element of judgement is required; and this is exercised by means of risk assessments, which will return different results for different types of enterprise. There are some common themes in every organization, and these are highlighted here, along with some of the underlying legal and regulatory requirements.

- *Data protection:* all organizations have to comply with the 1998 Data Protection Act, which came into effect in 2000. Do you know what your responsibilities for this are? Into this category also comes the Regulation of Investigatory Powers Act 2000 (RIP), which specifies who can take responsibility for the interception, monitoring and investigation of incidents; this is of particular relevance to organizations that need to determine who had access to any information held or processed electronically. Use of email and telephone-call monitoring procedures by an employer of its staff is covered by this RIP legislation.

- *Business continuity:* all organizations need to protect their equipment, software and data from intentional and unintentional loss. Do you have a plan to show how your business operates when key information goes missing? Business continuity in a 24×7×52 business environment is far more complex than having a disaster recovery plan involving cold standby facilities – for if you are an online retailer handling £2500 revenue *a minute*, can the business cashflow survive a 36-hour restore period? And will your customers accept this, even if the management do?

- *Internet threats:* anyone with PC-based systems and/or internet access is vulnerable to information being lost or rendered inaccessible due to a virus. This can also seriously affect service stability – it is estimated that 1 in every 212 emails sent in 2005 contained a virus. And if this wasn't bad enough, it is estimated by the author that the percentage of spam handled by ISPs grew from 2.3 per cent in June 2002 to 55 per cent in June 2003 and has remained at this level ever since, with over 1 per cent of this including viruses. Courts of law can use emails as formal records of the company for which you work, which is why email messages are frequently requested by the police. We can see that the email is often more deadly than the mail.

- *Denial of service:* although this is most often interpreted as being a sustained bombardment of your website, denial of service can be achieved in other ways, often inadvertently, if your network is not in a closed user group or has not been designed to use alternative routing and you get cut off from the outside world. This happens – and if you do online business, then you're out of it until the service is restored and tested.

- *Theft and loss of assets:* the growth in the number of laptops and other mobile devices means that both the hardware and information contained on them can and do go missing. Would you be happy if it was your medical records that were left behind on the bus? Or that your tax return was being examined by your competitors? Security is a deeply personal issue as well as one of corporate embarrassment – witness the many high-profile information leaks in recent years, especially through carelessness.

ISO 17799 and ISO 27001 together offer a comprehensive control framework for security management and interlock with ISO/IEC 20000. As has been described already, the security requirements of ISO/IEC 20000 are discharged by adherence to the code of practice and specification offered by

ISO 17799 and ISO 27001, which is why they are capable of being managed in an integrated manner.

Service and security synergy

This chapter has already asserted that there is significant synergy between the disciplines of security management and service management. If this is made obvious by a few examples, such as disaster management, then it can readily be seen how close the disciplines are. However, it is important not to take the leap towards organizational synergy without considering an important aspect of governance – segregation of duties. IT staff with deep technical skills are those who have the means, and arguably the time, to hack into systems for their own ends, and it is necessary to establish effective monitoring and control procedures to ensure that they don't. This may be more difficult when everyone is under the same management umbrella but, given that the benefits of synergy can outweigh the drawbacks, self-policing, assuming suitable external oversight and effective access control systems, becomes possible even in the most highly regulated organizations. All good ideas start off with either a feasibility study or a visionary statement. There are a number of ways in which the security management regime appropriate to your organization can be determined and a survey, taking no more than a few hours to complete, to assess conformance to ISO 17799 is a very good start. Management of security can be made cost effective if taken alongside a service improvement programme where the changes can be dovetailed; the author has seen this approach work well in practice.

If the most effective way of delivering high-quality services alongside robust operational KPIs and security appropriate for the business that never closes is being sought, then consider making security management part of the IT service improvement programme. This has been seen to offer savings of about 10 per cent of the cost of having separate teams, while also delivering better customer service.

SUPPLY CHAIN MANAGEMENT

Supply chain management is not just about how to manage an outsourcing contract. Although it is vital that the supply chain is managed properly, managing the provision of service based on diverse sources is considerably more important than managing a single supplier contract. IT outsourcing became topical again in the 1990s, long after computer bureaux had gone out of fashion as a result of the resurgence in corporate identity. The driver for outsourcing in the 1990s wasn't economy of scale or mass data preparation and entry but the management of complexity and responsiveness to customer needs, which many in-house IT organizations had failed to understand – or the agility needed to do these properly had become embroiled in company politics. Giving the task to an external services company was seen as a way of breaking both the competency and the political barriers to progress, even if the solution came at a similar cost, but this is where some fundamental assumptions started to go adrift. The first of these was that IT could be managed as an adjunct to business operations and in isolation to activities elsewhere in the company – which is now very obviously what it cannot be. Second, it was assumed that one company – an industry major – would take on the delivery of IT services for a term of 5, 7 or even 10 years, and yet many tears have been shed over mid-term divorce proceedings where the original deal could not cater for business changes over such a long period. Stability of supply may be an important factor, but not when it proves impractical to move the relationship onwards. Third, deals were struck with IT suppliers immediately before key business process changes that negated the sourcing model used to justify the scope of deal that had been agreed only a couple of months previously.

Unless the IT operation has already been outsourced, companies will buy products and services from companies they regard as most suitable for their needs. This is often on a 'best-of-breed' basis, which pays scant regard to the post-acquisition issues associated with integration. Technical fit is not as important to effective service delivery as process integration, and tools that pass data between themselves are far better than superior but standalone products. As an illustration, the IT marketplace has become significantly fragmented in the past 10 years, with the decline in the number of hardware suppliers being more than compensated for by the increase in the number of network and service providers, many of which are start-up companies. This leads to a confusing supply chain and one that demands more effort from the service aggregator than ever before, when larger companies could historically be relied upon to integrate products into a coherent service.

The weakest link

Regardless of individual product credentials, the key point to bear in mind when sourcing products and services is that they all have to work together to meet the intended purpose. Any one of these products can break the service chain and render the total investment invalid, the principle of the weakest link being a key point to remember. Most outsourcing deals acknowledge this and allow customers to manage their own service quality, but this comes at a price – anything up to 10 per cent of the contract value, which is rarely taken into business case justifications compared with the savings. Even if service integration is an in-house activity, the requirement to manage end-to-end service is often not recognized. It has been estimated that half of UK websites are not managed by IT departments and, of these, many have no operational status monitoring either – raising the question about who exactly is accountable for managing service quality once a customer connects over the internet.

The weakest link in many service operations is the management process. Database operations are generally well catered for, as are individual systems, but the element typically not as well controlled is the overall framework. This manifests itself by the IT department taking into account only individual applications and service elements rather than the overall view the customer receives, and this leads to surprises in terms of how the customer view compares with that of the service provider. This mismatch is best addressed by taking a service as opposed to a system view, as described in Chapter 3. This is where the responsibility is shared between the IT department and third-party suppliers, which many organizations fail to appreciate. Managing a supply chain across organizational boundaries requires a real process orientation as well as a degree of cooperation not normally envisaged when elements of service are put out to tender. This is the big difference between outsourcing and out-tasking, as the latter places a greater responsibility on the in-house department to manage the overall service delivery. Figure 7.4 shows an example of how in-house and third-party tasks should be organized, based on the specification within ISO/IEC 20000, to deliver a service to a customer who should view that service as seamless. If the service expectation is not met, then the responsibility should always lie with the IT department, which has a responsibility to manage the logistics process and their subcontractors – the customer should not be exposed to this issue.

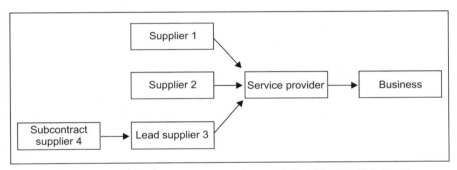

FIGURE 7.4 *Supply chain management as defined in ISO/IEC 20000*

Crown jewels

IT service providers have a role to manage the diverse set of tools, value-added products and outsourced components that typically make up today's service offering. An effective way of doing this is to consider carefully what competencies the service organization needs to retain and what it ought to rely on other companies to provide. This concept can best be illustrated by the model in Figure 7.5, which shows how a (fictitious) restaurant owner might organize the delivery of meals to the restaurant's customers. This concept is known as a hub-and-spoke operation as a means of defining the crown jewels, which are those elements of the service chain that can be outsourced as opposed to those that have to be retained. These elements vary according to the organization concerned, since the spectrum of service can be anywhere between fully in-house supplied to fully outsourced, but the same principles apply – a decision needs to be made about what needs to be managed within and what does not. The hub in this model contains the retained expertise, whereas the spokes are the elements that have been outsourced and interface back into the hub through clearly defined agreements.

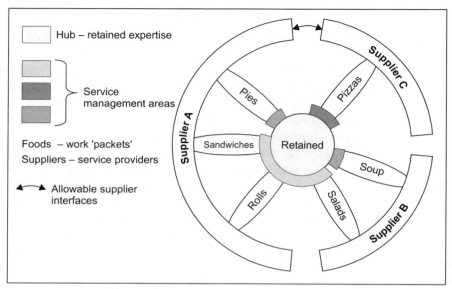

FIGURE 7.5   *Example of hub and spoke as a way of deciding what to retain*

There are some obvious elements that – in the author's view – should be part of the crown jewels for most organizations:

- *End user contact:* outsourcing the helpdesk means the parent company loses control of customer contact, a key moment of truth (MOT) issue. Disintermediation of the customer can allow another company to take the place of underlying service provider with minimal forewarning.

- *Technology choice:* allowing someone else to choose a service technology means you may get what they can make most margin on and not necessarily what is best for the type of service you offer. Service management technologies must be capable of providing a true end-user view of service and not just be best-of-breed products.

- *Process compliance:* the way in which all the products and subcomponents work together is a key competency that the service provider needs to retain. The weakest link often occurs when there is split responsibility for elements of the service process, so retain the management competency and accountability in just one place.

Defining the right crown jewels, managing the supply chain correctly and understanding the rationale behind every sourcing decision will enable IT service providers to deliver to their customer expectations. This should be the case even when it goes wrong, which is where management accountability is needed – not only to manage the recovery but also to manage the customers. This is where the service chain really does come home to roost, since an often overheard excuse is to blame a subcontractor. Best-practice service takes no account of individual component performance and, unless the customer specifically insisted on managing a certain subcontractor directly, blaming them ducks your own responsibility. Another aspect of service accountability is in the interface with the customer, where they may be responsible themselves for something going wrong. If the service is managed such that the customer can adversely impact service quality, especially for other people as well as themselves, then there is a problem that will only get worse, since customers have ever increasing expectations of availability, performance and timeliness, and it is usually the provider that has to deal with such issues.

One good example of this is the provision of desktop services. Although it would seem obvious that a large corporate organization would understand that a new starter needs to be provided with a workstation, it is remarkable how often this is not available on time. The ordering, build and installation process for a new PC can often take weeks and involve many different staff to achieve, which is clearly nonsense. The erratic supply of workstations is one of the main gripes heard by customers about how they are treated by corporate IT departments. Effective supply chain management based on the crown jewels principle will have decided how best to organize and sequence the work between in-house and supplier resources and will build a process to manage this to a repeatable standard. Figure 7.6 shows a real example of a process designed to provide a PC to the desk within 72 hours of requisition.

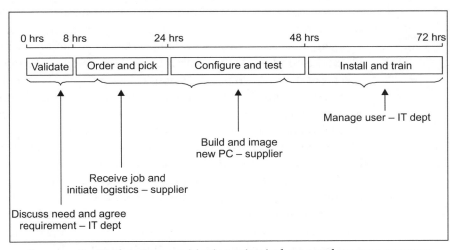

FIGURE 7.6 *Workstation provisioning using in-house and contract resources*

It is relatively easy to achieve a three-day turnaround of something in a cardboard box, but this is not what the 72-hour example shown in Figure 7.6 is planned to deliver. What it means in practice is that:

- the customer is provided with a slick means of requisitioning what he or she needs and the means by which to account for that request in the budget;

- the commodity portfolio is structured to provide a range of fit-for-purpose solutions rather than a lengthy and bewildering shopping list of products;

- the workstation is packed, imaged and shipped through an arrangement with a logistics provider that offers 24-hour capability;

- any network changes are planned in advance of delivery and a patching schedule provided for the installation technician;

- the installation technician is empowered to do everything to commission the workstation in one visit, leaving the device connected and working;

- the user is given familiarization training by the installer to ensure the user knows the basics about how the software and/or hardware can be used.

This class of service breaks a number of classical IT boundaries – involving the networks department, the training department and the financial management systems. The issue is not, however, that this is too hard to do but that the cost of providing service in this manner is a lot cheaper than doing it the longer way because it involves fewer people and gets the job done faster, and so the customer is more productive. By teaming with a logistics provider that can offer pick and delivery services round the clock means the 72-hour elapsed time can involve up to nine working days' effort – which is actually about the number of office days most IT departments take to provide such a service at present. Since the 72-hour rule was first proposed, it has become apparent in many FTSE 100 companies that customer satisfaction is not taken into account in the provisioning cycle, which is why it is disappointing to find that IT departments struggle with this most simple and repetitive of tasks. Those teams that have recognized the elegance of breaking down internal barriers to effective service have been rewarded by happier customers, better supplier relations and lower costs – as well as improved staff satisfaction through dealing more effectively and reliably. As well as the obvious benefits, there are political benefits – because a consistent and effective provisioning process also mitigates frustrated customers from going down to the local PC store and getting what they need and then asking IT to incorporate it into the service catalogue after the event.

Another benefit of having such a streamlined delivery system is that incremental software upgrades can also be provided on user request. Having a tightly controlled scripted delivery system means that a software package can be requisitioned and downloaded on demand, because the procurement system will already have been geared to cater for customer demand management. The issue of users downloading new software – for instance, to do project management or graphics editing – can lead to training and familiarization problems, but again the demand management process can take this into account by automatically booking the requestor on to a suitable course if the package is a new installation and adding the cost of this to the authority that the requisitioner needs to provide. Such an arrangement involves establishing call-off arrangements with training providers – or an in-house function – to ensure that value is being achieved through best use of such new software. As discussed in Chapter 6, techniques such as ECDL and INVEST are available to help with this process and, on the basis that historical requirements for new packages suggest that future demand will always be strong, the provision of hardware, software and training services on demand can be forecast and organized in advance of the need.

Code of best practice

Effective supply chain management needs a good relationship between the supplier and the customer in order for the transaction to work properly; this has been the main theme of this book throughout. However, such relationships often break down once a contract is involved, with both the customer and the supplier developing entrenched views about the product or service being delivered. This is as true in the public and not-for-profit sectors as it is in the traditional commercial world, and the scapegoat is usually the supplier because they are being paid to do the work. This is unfortunate and sometimes unfair – the supplier can be only as good as the customer will allow the supplier to be, especially in regard to the specification of a service. In recognition of this, a code of best practice has been developed by Intellect, a trade organization that represents 1000 companies in the IT, telecommunications and electronics industries in the UK, in order to improve the supply experience. Although this code was developed specifically for public-sector customers, and in particular for government procurement, it has wide applicability to any IT supply relationship and should be regarded as a major source of reference for any business intending to accede to world-class status. The aim of the code is to facilitate a more mature acquisition and delivery relationship that offers benefits to both customers and suppliers, by avoiding either of them having to take entrenched and unhelpful positions in the delivery of a major service. This can be summarized as providing:

- *for the customers:* a greater certainty of successful delivery and better value from IT-enabled programmes;
- *for the suppliers:* more successful and sustainable business for a fair rate of return.

The objective of the code is to help raise the standards of professionalism throughout the IT supplier community. The code describes the standards of best practice that all IT suppliers working in the public sector should endeavour to achieve. The code sets out the principles of best practice through a series of commitments that focus on the role of the supplier but that recognize that they will operate most effectively when the values described in these commitments are complemented by the approach taken by the customer to the supply relationship. The ten commitments are set out below; access to the more detailed code of best practice and supporting information is available from Intellect at www.intellectuk.org.

THE TEN COMMITMENTS

Commitment 1 We will strive to build and maintain an effective relationship with the customer, founded on mutual trust and openness, with a clear understanding of each other's goals and interests.

Commitment 2 We will make every reasonable effort to ensure we develop and agree with the customer a full and robust understanding of the requirement and its broader business context as a firm foundation for our proposals.

Commitment 3 We will be ready to offer constructive challenge whenever we believe improvements could usefully be made to the shaping or delivery of a programme, with the aim of ensuring an improved solution.

Commitment 4 We will only bid what we believe we can deliver with a high degree of confidence and on business models that can be sustained for the planned life of the programme.

Commitment 5 We will declare all relevant assumptions that we make during the course of a programme (and make clear their implications), in particular those that relate to information or services provided by the customer.

Commitment 6 We will ensure that all aspects of the programme are managed to a high degree of professionalism, using an agreed methodology and, wherever appropriate, with a clear focus on the delivery of business benefits.

Commitment 7 We will rigorously identify, analyse and manage risks and we will seek to agree solutions with the customer that offer the best ownership and risk mitigation strategy.

Commitment 8	We will provide sufficient transparency through-out the supply chain that subcontractors can shape their offerings and manage their work appropri-ately and the customer has suitable visibility at all levels.
Commitment 9	We will only nominate individuals for specific roles or as team members whom we judge to have the necessary authority, skills and experience and are expected to be available. Their contribution to cus-tomer satisfaction and successful programme deliv-ery will be encouraged and recognized.
Commitment 10	We will encourage our staff to acquire and main-tain appropriate professional standards and indi-vidual competencies. We will work towards a com-mon and agreed framework for specific roles and associated competencies.

Reproduced by kind permission of Intellect.

It can be seen that adherence to these commitments involves much more than a procurement or legal services department can offer and will therefore complement any formal contract process. It is instructive to put into prac-tice these commitments and to observe the effect they have on both parties to the relationship, since it does challenge conventional supplier manage-ment. Although a supplier may routinely claim to do most, or all, of these things, it can be a different matter when they proactively use the code as a means of communicating their intentions in detail with the customer. It is equally instructive to observe the effect that techniques such as construct-ive challenge, subcontractor transparency and risk management have on a traditional customer base that may be used to managing by fear, threat and contractual fine print and not by cooperation.

Although this code was written with the public sector in mind, it is of relev-ance to any type of IT supply situation, especially in the commercial sector, where it is becoming increasingly rare to encounter a written specification. This offers a different kind of problem to a deal where the deliverables and terms of supply are set out clearly, because in fact the only documentation that exists is that produced by the supplier. This trend is increasing rapidly for two reasons – first, service is intangible and therefore the customer does not necessarily know what is needed; second, customers are often not skilled in documentation and specification and have no ready access to procure-ment skills. This is especially true in the small and medium-sized enterprise (SME) sector, but it is also in evidence in larger organizations where budget management has been devolved to line management. IT suppliers can, therefore, use the code of best practice to guide their dealings with the customer throughout the lifetime of the transaction and hence ensure that the result is mutually satisfactory.

ASSET AND CONFIGURATION MANAGEMENT

Discussions on the management of IT assets are often enough to bore even the most ardent systems manager – until 'that' event happens. But what is 'that', and why should such an event act as a wake-up call to do something? Well, 'that' event could be notification of a visit from the Federation Against Software Theft (FAST). Or a call from your director's PA to say that he's lost his laptop and can he have another one with exactly the same configuration. Or it might be that the ERP application needs a patch distributing to all workstations – immediately.

These challenges highlight the need to manage IT assets in a highly professional manner, which is at the very heart of enterprise management. If the role of the reader is within a medium to large enterprise, then the situations outlined at the start of this section will be very real. They should all be in a day's work for IT departments in every sector – expect that such events often precipitate significant, frantic activity for the simple reason that we don't always know *who* has got *what*, or even *where* it is. Companies with fixed asset registers will keep records of their hardware assets at the time of purchase, but asset ledgers as part of a financial accounting package are not usually accessible to IT managers and are updated infrequently. Such fixed asset registers do not reflect the technical detail that IT managers need to effectively manage 'those' events referred to earlier.

So, how much of a real issue is asset and configuration management today? The answer is self-evident to any company with licensed software, with people who lose laptops or that has a large user base – it's the difference between being able to satisfy the need without diversion of effort away from other tasks. And then being able to do it again tomorrow, and the day after that.

Any enterprise with a sizeable installed base of PC workstations will recognize that operational complexity increases disproportionately with the numbers involved, and in many organizations, churn rates – the number of workstations that need upgrading, moving or refreshing – can exceed 30 per cent per year, with dynamic organizations experiencing anything up to 100 per cent churn.

So what can be done to exert the appropriate amount of management to this aspect of IT? There is no shortage of standards and specifications covering asset and configuration management – witness the ITIL treatises on this subject as well as the new international standard ISO/IEC 20000, which mandates process compliance in a number of areas in order to achieve accreditation. Configuration management is central to the attainment of

ISO/IEC 20000, as it was for its BS 150000 predecessor, although this is not the only recognized standard for configuration management, since ISO 10007 has existed for some time in the manufacturing and logistics world.

But IT is different!

The personnel manager in your company knows exactly how many people work in the organization, where they are based and how much to pay them each month. Similarly, the fleet manager keeps accurate records of what company and pool cars he or she is responsible for, who has them and when they are going to be sold, upgraded or moved between departments. These people expect to manage the assets under their control as a normal part of their day job, unlike IT departments, which rarely know exactly how many bits of inventory they control or from where the current 'owner' is working.

We also expect new roads, railways, sewers and telephone services to be mapped accurately and records kept about their maintenance – so why should IT claim to be any different? The same issues arise with software, since this is as much of an asset as the more obviously visible hardware and has to be paid for either by the number of licenses needed or by the capability of the kit on which it is hosted. If a company with 10,000 employees can keep track of everyone, pay them on time and legally keep a fleet of vehicles on the road, then IT has to be up to the challenge of managing the corporate information assets they use to at least the same standard. Much of the blame for poor asset management can be attributed to the way in which IT assets are acquired, either on a project-by-project basis or by end-user purchasing, although neither of these reasons is an allowable excuse under current IT governance rules. An effective asset governance regime will exhibit some fundamental management principles:

- IT assets belong to the company, not the employee or department.
- No personal data should be held on PCs.
- Access is blocked to non-corporate data such as eBay and MP3 sites.
- All software must be registered on an auditable database.
- Network patch automation tools should be used to record all changes.
- Every asset is uniquely registered on the network and is known to IT.

The only reason that IT is different is that it expects to be so. However, the rules have changed and a discipline for IT asset management is now needed.

A common problem in this respect is that many companies inadvertently allow staff access to music sites, from where – assuming payment is made – legal copies of tunes can be downloaded. However, storing these on company servers gives rise to the problem of copyright theft and the potential for law suits in connection with the illegal distribution of MP3 files – such as in the case of Integrated Information Systems in Arizona, which settled out of court for $1 million to avoid prosecution for copyright infringement by employees who accessed music files through their servers. Effective asset management policies will avoid the potential for such embarrassing situations and maximize legitimate IT capacity. Best practice in this respect is published by the International Federation of the Recording Industry (IFPI) based in London, which makes available a copyright use and security guide that explains the policy on use of copyright material and which has developed sample memos that can be sent to staff covering the legal, commercial and moral implications of music downloads at work.

Configuration management at the heart of control

IT needs to ensure that every computing asset is effectively controlled, managed and operated according to the environment in which it is used. This can be done most simply by implementing asset and configuration control at senior management level, linked to other key disciplines such as change and release management as defined by ITIL and ISO/IEC 20000. This is administered by tools such as a configuration management database (CMDB), which is described conceptually in Figure 7.7, together with its key attributes.

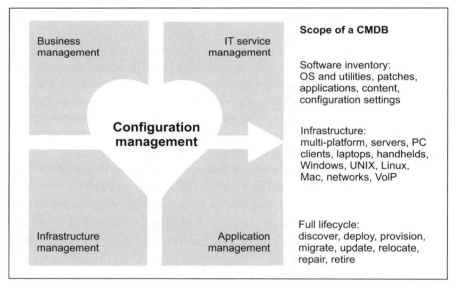

FIGURE 7.7   *Configuration management at the heart of IT*

This type of control regime leads to a number of significant benefits, including:

- tighter control of IT assets, leading to reduced purchasing;
- better awareness of software and distributed licence management;
- shorter time to achieve repair, replacement or upgrade;
- better audit and regulatory compliance;
- improved IT and user staff time utilization during change;
- control over staff activities and reduction in corporate liabilities.

Effective asset control and configuration management is essential in order to gain ISO/IEC 20000 accreditation. But it would be wrong to assume that all this can be done without giving rise to concerns, not least of which will come from users, who will see increased IT control as inhibiting their freedom to do whatever they like with 'their' PC. However, in the same way that the fleet manager does not allow unauthorized modifications to company cars, neither should the IT manager allow similar infringements to corporate information facilities. The advantages of the IT manager over the fleet counterpart lie in the tools that are available to manage, audit and control the asset base – and if staff still conspire to circumvent them, then the personnel manager is available to offer support for disciplinary proceedings. A case study into the need for a CMDB is appropriate here.

CASE STUDY – UTILITIES COMPANY

This nationwide organization had a team looking after a PC asset register, which recorded the acquisition of all workstations and to whom they were allocated. Associated with this was a software licensing arrangement that ensured that all workstations had an up-to-date software build and that all copies of the software in use were acquired appropriately and could be accounted for. This represented a good level of basic control and formed the basis for a competent asset register – except that it was not clear how many PCs were actually still used in the organization. When the records were analysed, it was seen that out of the 3781 workstations listed in the register, 347 had not had any contact with the network that year – and their current whereabouts was unknown. As the company had operations based across the UK, this was a worrying situation with regard to information and data leakage as well as providing a potential cost overhead – the company was paying 9 per cent more for software licences than it had hardware on which the software was to be run. Of the 347 'missing' workstations, 69 were laptops, which could well have been lost or stolen – no-one knew of their whereabouts. Even if these had not been connected to the network because they were always being used in the field, their virus scanners would be many months out of date and the software revision levels would not have reflected the frequent changes to corporate builds.

Situations as outlined in this case study are regrettably commonplace. Good record-keeping alone is not enough; this has to be enforced by systems and automation to mandate control. Automated discovery tools to detect when a workstation comes into contact with the network is a good first step but is not sufficient on its own to demonstrate best practice asset control, which is where emerging standards and technology will help.

Emerging standards and tools

A new ISO standard on software asset management (SAM) to complement ISO/IEC 20000 was published in mid-2006. This new standard, known as ISO

19770, was developed to provide an internationally agreed definition against which organizations can measure their policies and procedures to ensure good asset management quality. Following this standard, which for many professional service delivery organizations will also mean becoming formally accredited to it, will help IT departments achieve compliance with their legal and commercial obligations as well as demonstrating effective governance of software assets as part of an increasing focus on IT controls. SAM on its own will not satisfy ISO/IEC 20000 or deal with the problem of physical asset moves, changes and thefts. However, one technology that could be used to complement ISO 19770 is the deployment of radio frequency identification (RFID) tags on all moveable assets so they can be discovered without the need for physical hardware verification. More than 1.3 billion RFID tags were made in 2005. Such tags are now inexpensive to provide (about 10p for a passive tag), as are the various tracking devices needed to make use of the information provided by the tags.

RFID tags come in two types – active and passive. The passive variety responds only when in close contact with an RFID reader; these tags are increasingly being used by retailers for functions such as stock control. As they need no power supply, they can be incorporated into asset tags and labels in much the same way as a barcode. The advantage of the tags over barcodes is that the tag does not need to be seen to be read: it simply has to be within range – typically around 500 mm, even if something else is between the tag and the reader. Such tags operate in the ultra-high frequency (UHF) radio band above the frequencies used for radio microphones but below that for TV transmissions, a spectrum that has been reserved specifically for short-range radio transmission. The other type of RFID tag that is increasingly becoming available is the active type, which allows activation by a nearby reader and is capable of supporting write operations. Operating in the very high frequency (VHF) band, below that of commercial radio stations, active tags offer a much longer range, around 10 m, as they are battery-powered and can be used for dynamic inventory control. Examples of this type of tag can be found in manufacturing industries for controlling pallet movement about a factory and in distribution businesses to track the whereabouts of containers. The potential for RFID tags to support the next generation of configuration management systems is clearly open to exploitation, and would, assuming that appropriate readers had been installed in the doorways to the utility company described in the case study in this chapter, have explained exactly where the assets were – or confirmed that, in fact, they were no longer in use. An IT department that is capable of tracking its mobile workforce through RFID tags and that manages its software in accordance with ISO 19770 will be in control of its assets to the extent required for world class.

SUMMARY

- Use IT governance as a key management technique to establish and demonstrate effective control and compliance over service delivery.
- Treat information security as a companion to service delivery because they contain the same basic management principles.
- Establish the concept of federated working for service supply based on cooperation with suppliers that provide good logistics support and that can work within a supply framework based on the ten commitments.
- Treat asset and configuration management as seriously and as objectively as do personnel and fleet managers the assets under their control.
- Deploy new standards and techniques such as RFID tagging to improve the way in which assets are discovered, tracked and accounted for.

8 The end result

The previous chapters have covered different aspects of the way in which a service delivery organization needs to change in order to become world class. All of these aspects, even when taken in isolation, should have a beneficial effect on the outcomes that can be expected – but the benefit of combining them all into a coherent proposition is much more significant. This chapter draws together the various themes into a whole and provides operational targets in order to create a clearly defined goal. This set of targets cannot be achieved by using any one method on its own, since the areas of service to which they relate can interact, and a change made in one area of focus will adversely affect another. However, regardless of whether the achievements described in this chapter are met exactly or not, world-class service organizations all display a number of shared attributes:

- They provide a quantifiably high level of customer experience.
- Internal productivity and staff satisfaction are as good as can be achieved.
- Service delivery attainments are regularly benchmarked and reported.
- Internal politics and inefficiencies are rooted out to minimize interference with the achievement of a good customer experience.
- New service value propositions are continually being developed.
- Staff are skilled, trained, motivated and rewarded.

This may seem utopia and to represent an unachievable state, but this is not the case, as many FTSE 100 and unquoted larger corporations have developed along these lines and can demonstrate world class in action. Most of the third-party service providers specializing in outsourced service management have to adopt these techniques in order to stay competitive and therefore retain business; and if it is necessary for them, then it must be necessary for an in-house team as well. In-house service departments are competing either in reality or in terms of management judgements with third-party service providers and so need to be aware of the standards and achievements being offered in the commercial marketplace. The next section examines a range of quantified world-class service targets that typify the attainments of companies operating at the peak of their game.

WHAT REACHING WORLD CLASS WILL LOOK LIKE

Many references have been made in this book to the need to establish service management benchmarks and to track performance against the market. This is an imperative if an organization needs to know where it is on its service journey. Although this section does not provide a complete set of benchmark reference data, it does document the key parameters that a world-class delivery organization ought to be challenged to meet. The arrangement of these targets has been structured into three types of metric – an organizational design indicator (ODI), which are the factors that can be used to scale an IT function; critical success factors (CSF), which are those factors by which service delivery targets can be set; and key performance indicators (KPI), which are used as a measure of achievement against target.

These indicators are all based on practising organizations and so are both representative of the IT service industry today and achievable. There is no mention of any supporting technologies, since a number of products and tools are available to help organizations reach these targets, and this book is not concerned with product endorsement except by means of example. Tables 8.1 and 8.2 describe two types of indicator – management and operational. The management ratios are those around which an organization can be developed and sized, whereas the operational targets are those that a service delivery team should aim to satisfy.

TABLE 8.1   *Management indicators*

Note	Management indicator	Type of measure	Best practice	
1	Number of services variable staff needed to support size of user base	ODI	50 : 1	Ratio of user PCs to IT PC-related staff levels: 4000 users will need 80 staff to support and manage them properly
2	Number of technical specialists needed to support infrastructure	ODI	5.3/day	Measure of tier 3 productivity in clearing calls escalated from service management areas T1 and T2
3	Size of first-tier customer service support group	ODI	222 : 1	First point of contact – a tier 1 helpdesk team ratio expressed as users/IT
4	Number of applications supported per analyst	ODI	6 : 1	Systems per member of applications support team
5	Customer satisfaction results based on operational user surveys	KPI	≥ 80%	Score out of 100 needed to rate services at best-practice levels
6	Customer satisfaction results based on project managers surveyed	KPI	≥ 95%	Score out of 100 needed to rate services at best-practice levels
7	Customer satisfaction results based on strategic leadership group survey	KPI	100%	Score out of 100 needed to rate services at best-practice levels
8	Cost of delivery	CSF	£65	Cost per user per month for ITSM staffing
9	Staff satisfaction ratings	CSF	≥ 60%	Score out of 100 for service delivery staff satisfaction
		CSF	< 1.5%	Target sick absence rate
		CSF	< 5.0%	Target turnover rate

Note 1:   This does not cover every member of a services team, since many roles are independent of the number of users supported – for example, senior management or wide-area network (WAN) operation. The variable element of services staffing concerned directly with user management and support for the variety of systems used in organizations should be based on a ratio of 50 users to one IT professional, which includes helpdesk staff, desktop support, security administration, service managers and any others that vary

in proportion to the user base. This ratio is for use within a corporate rather than a public IT service offering.

Note 2: Specialists supporting delivery of services should be able to work on the basis of reference metrics for their productivity. The reference point used here is that each member of tier 3 technical support functions should be dealing with 5.3 jobs per person-day, which can be determined by analysis of both current and historical fault levels based on referrals from the helpdesk or by analysis of work logs.

Note 3: Best-practice tier 1 support levels for users with PC-based workstations are calculated on the basis of 222 users to each tier 1 analyst. For example, a 4000-user corporate IT organization could expect to need 18 helpdesk analysts, assuming the supporting tools and skills were provided to them, covering an extended day from 8 am to 6 pm and allowing for holidays and training – this is a net, rather than a gross figure.

Note 4: Another productivity measure for a complex multinational organization concerns systems support staff. It does not matter whether these staff are in service delivery or systems development; the metric shown here is that one full-time member of support is needed for every six live supported systems. So, an organization with 240 operational applications could expect to deploy 40 people to support them and provide minor enhancements – up to a maximum of 10 person-days per occasion, which represents a practical cut-off point between project work and the support role.

Notes 5–7: Customer satisfaction measures need to play a key role in the management of IT. Three such measures are relevant here, the first being that operational users, the majority of staff who use IT services on a day-by-day basis, should score service delivery at a satisfaction rating of 80 per cent or higher against objective service criteria. The second measure is a higher standard, being relevant to the management and delivery of projects and 95 per cent is suggested here. The final measure is that of strategic alignment, where the most senior organization decision makers should rate 100 per cent of IT's efforts as being relevant to commercial success.

Note 8: This figure is taken from industry pricing models that are known to offer best-practice financial performance. There is a ± 10 per cent range on this figure, depending on location and scale of the operation under support, but it can be used as a guide to define the cost consumption of IT service delivery. The figure includes all ITSM staffing costs, including training, travel, National Insurance (NI) and pension contributions, but it does not include non-payroll operational costs, since these vary significantly with the scale and capitalization polices used.

Note 9: Staff satisfaction measures are important, since high-performing services organizations need to have a motivated and committed workforce in order to achieve the levels of customer satisfaction reported above. The first-choice employer status will lead to a first-choice supplier result if service delivery staff have a satisfaction rating of 60 per cent or above from surveys taken concerning communication and engagement on a world-class programme, processes and technology. Aligned to satisfaction with communication will be other key indicators of staff satisfaction, notably sick absence and turnover, and the figures shown here are typical of those encountered in high-performing motivated delivery teams.

TABLE 8.2 *Operational indicators*

Note	Operational indicator	Type of measure	Best practice	
10	Incidents generated per user	CSF	< 5%	Users reporting problems per day
11	Calls abandoned	KPI	< 7%	Users ringing off before call is answered
12	Time to answer	KPI	90% ≤ 30 secs	IT helpdesk norm when taken with an 80% closure rate
13	Fault calls closed	CSF	> 95%	Faults recorded, handled and cleared within agreed SLA
14	Calls handled per analyst	ODI	40	Per working person-day for calls being resolved
15	Calls closed at first touch	KPI	80%	Fault resolved by desk with no repeat call and within SLA
16	Delivery of work orders – new requests for service	CSF	3 days	Time taken to deliver, e.g. new desktop to user
17	Ability to execute change	CSF	99.5%	Success rate for change implementation

Note 10: World-class organizations should be looking to minimize the volume of service requests in order to provide adequate user productivity and to best manage the costs of IT support. This measure is one that offers a balance between the cost of developing good service and that of delivering it. The metric includes incidents relating to password resets and work orders and so represents a balanced workload, not just fault calls. It is a total figure for IT, based on the premise that all support requests should be recorded. If there are any requests that circumvent the process, they should be picked up and compared with this metric in order to avoid miscounting.

Note 11: Call queues need to be short in order to sustain an acceptable level of abandoned attempts, which lead to user dissatisfaction, user-initiated workarounds and the potential for longer-term service problems. With the move to user self-service and voicemail, however – which do not use the same metrics – call queues need to reflect complex queries.

Note 12: Time to answer statistics for an internal helpdesk, as opposed to an external call centre operated by an IT services company, should reflect the other metrics used in these sections. The purpose of a service desk is to resolve incidents and not just *handle calls* relating to them, the primary performance metric is that 80 per cent of calls should be fixed in real time, which often militates against fast call pickup, since taking more time on each call to resolve the issue may mean slightly longer waiting times for each caller. This performance figure is set to compensate for that.

Note 13: All calls passed to a service desk should be logged, analysed, resolved and closed. There will be some calls, however, that, although routed to an IT service desk, cannot sensibly be logged and analysed, the < 5 per cent metric allows for these. The > 95 per cent target should be used as a CSF for closure.

Note 14: An IT service desk manned by support analysts provided with access to historical fault data, technical training aligned to the complexity of the systems under support and the right supporting technology should handle 40 calls per person per day – a rate of about 5 calls per analyst per hour. This is not just call handling, however: when allied with note 12, this means that 40 calls a day will be resolved and closed on the service desk.

Note 15: Call closure on the helpdesk is an area where some interpretation is needed. Although it is laudable to have a high level of fault calls resolved while the user is online, this metric becomes problematic if the time taken for this resolution exceeds the time that it would take for someone to visit that user and resolve their issue directly. The analogy to be borne in mind here is that of a car breakdown call to a motoring organization, where the operator will carry out a number of checks with the distressed driver and schedule a breakdown vehicle callout if the problem cannot be diagnosed within the first few minutes. As the response time for the breakdown vehicle is usually only 45 minutes, the elapsed time before the driver gets an appropriate intervention gets worse the longer a dialogue with the operator continues. It is good practice to decide whether to invoke deskside support within the first two minutes of an inbound call and for that support to be provided to users on main corporate sites within 15 minutes – and for a fix to be provided and the call closed without further user involvement and usually within 30 minutes. This requires strong logistics management of deskside support and third-party maintenance providers by helpdesk and skills at both tier 1 and tier 2 levels in order to support this. The 80 per cent target is to show how many calls should be handled by tier 1/tier 2 helpdesk analysts with the user in real time and before escalation to tier 3.

Note 16: Satisfaction of new work requests is one of the real tests of IT service orientation. Best practice mandates that 100 per cent of all work will be done within an agreed time and for 95 per cent of new installations to be completed within 72 hours of request – including delivery of a configured workstation as well as any network patching, ID creation and initial user training.

Note 17: The ability to execute changes to live services is another key determinant of IT management capability. An effective change management regime will ensure not only that changes are handled through a known and accepted process but that the changes do what they are designed to do – and not cause any regression failures either. Less than 0.5% of changes made by a best-practice organization that uses a mixture of test rigs, parameter-based systems designs and highly scripted release mechanisms should fail.

DEVELOPING AN IMPROVEMENT PROGRAMME

Setting out on the journey to world class is not only a case of taking the targets shown above and setting them as objectives for the delivery team. By deciding to accede to world class, the whole IT organization needs to understand what it means to reach this level of competency and what it takes to stay there – effort for which is also required. Without simply repeating the advice contained in earlier chapters, the best way to approach the definition of an improvement programme is as suggested below:

Step 1:   Understand how current levels of IT service support your customer needs both now and into the future. This will provide the drivers for change based on a customer viewpoint.

Step 2:   Perform a gap analysis on this result against world class by means of either an external benchmark or possibly using the three types of management indicator given earlier in this chapter as an initial phase. This will provide a view on how close current performance and management levels are to industry standards.

Step 3:   Work out both the cost and benefit of improving service standards to those shown by benchmarking. There will undoubtedly be tangible as well as intangible components of both the price and the reward, and it is important to factor these into the benefits equation. Costing this over a term – say 5 years as a minimum – is important because the programme will inevitably be cost-loaded at the start and benefits-loaded at the end. This will lead to a formal business case for change.

Step 4:   Engage a competent change manager to oversee the change rather than expect the existing team to make the change as well as deliver everyday operations. It is difficult to drain a swamp at the same time as fighting the alligators within it, and so it is important to separate the roles, while at the same time recognizing that the change manager will be viewed with suspicion by the incumbent team. This can be addressed in a number of ways, most significant of which is either by using an external resource or – the route that is recommended – by bringing in someone with a competency identified as missing during the gap analysis. This person would, on completion of the programme, then move to a line role in the new delivery organization, which means they cannot be regarded as having an agenda other than one of creating success for the team.

Step 5:   Be realistic about the pace of change that can be achieved. The change programme will not be the only initiative under way and, apart from keeping current services running, the delivery team may also be faced with putting some significant new systems into live operation. A rule of thumb under these circumstances is that a practical limit of achievement for a change programme is 15 per cent per annum. If the gap analysis carried out in step 2 shows that current service performance is 70 per cent of world class, then the programme will take two years to complete. There is a common misconception, unfortunately often spread by consultants with a vested interest in selling services, that change can happen more quickly than that with more external support. Although external support is often valuable, it is of most use in the facilitation rather than the delivery phase because the customer experience, that fallible and fickle determinant of how good you really can be, does not take kindly to consultancy delivery and many otherwise worthy programmes have failed to deliver the expected benefits because of a misalignment of competency and ongoing accountability. The maxim of doing it to yourself is better than having it done to you is important in this regard.

These five steps are an indication of the approach to be taken rather than a definitive plan regardless of circumstance. Having gone through this process many times, the author understands that each organization is different whereas every organization is simultaneously similar – and the way in which a change programme is organized matters a great deal. The five steps represent a distillation of an approach that has been proved to work across every industry sector and at a pace consistent with the ability of customers to absorb such change, which is also a key factor.

MAINTAINING TRANSFORMATIONAL VALUE

Although a project approach to the accession to world class is an effective approach, the work involved does not stop once the desired status has been reached. This is at variance with the approach taken to traditional projects but it is no different from what ought to happen in any transformation initiative. Getting to where you want to be is one objective, but staying where you need to be is another objective, albeit linked inextricably to the first. Maintaining the status that has been the result of, perhaps, many months or even years of work and the investment of time and money is often overlooked in change projects. As a reference, it is advisable to look to the manufacturing sector for guidance. Companies that develop and market high-technology products typically reinvest 15 per cent of their sales revenues on research and development for the next generation of products – some firms will go even higher than this. The reason they do this is to maintain a market position and show that not only is the next generation of products better than the previous one but that they are still innovating. This is exactly the position that applies to service offerings as well and therefore helps to validate the whole Service Accession Model introduced in Chapter 1. What can be classed as excellent service today may not be so regarded in the future and it is important to maintain an investment in service transformation long after any enabling project has been completed. This continuous reinvestment process has two aims:

- keeping on the high ground once a transformation project completes;
- ensuring that IT services track increasing customer expectations.

Keeping on the high ground

Maintaining the position is a relatively easy situation to address because both the management effort involved and the incremental costs are low. It is more important at this stage to be able to recognize that maintenance effort is required, akin to that of any complex machine such as a car or a piece of hospital diagnostic equipment, in order to maintain it at the desired performance. The cost of maintenance should be regarded as being proportional to the value of the initial investment – for example, if a car costs £60,000, then its owner may expect to spend 2 per cent per annum on maintenance; similarly, if another car costs £15,000, then the owner may also expect to spend about 2 per cent each year on its upkeep. The actual cost of maintenance will be different because of the value of the initial purchase cost of the car, but the proportion – in this example, 2 per cent – will be the same. In the case of service transformation, the value of achieving a defined end position will have come at a price, and although this should have resulted in a highly efficient and cost-effective delivery operation this position needs to be maintained, otherwise it will degrade. Service transformation initiatives have a shelf life similar to that of fruit and, unless renewed constantly, they quickly become stale. It was shown in Chapter 6 that a level of investment is necessary in terms of the development in customer skills in order to maintain an appropriate competency in the use of advanced computer services; this concept is equally applicable to the overall service proposition. Figure 8.1 illustrates the investment cycle that is, regrettably, often experienced in companies following a significant investment in service transformation.

The level of investment necessary to maximize the go-live state as shown in Figure 8.1 can be quite significant – for a company low down on the accession model and without much enabling technology already in place, this could amount to several millions of pounds or dollars; a company in the later stages of development, however, may not need more than a fraction of this to get to the same state. However, unless the maximum value position is actively maintained, then the investment taken to reach this point will gradually be eroded at about the same rate that it takes to accede to it in the first place – 15 per cent per annum. If a transformation programme has cost, say, £1 million to implement, then it will lose £150,000 of that value in each subsequent year unless the status is maintained proactively. Experience of more than a dozen recent service transformation projects suggests that the cost of maintaining

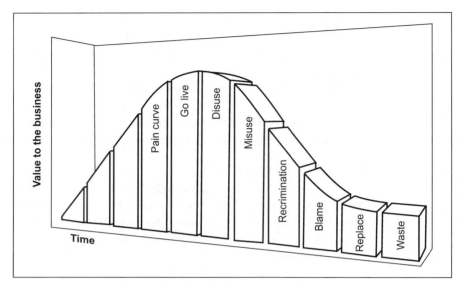

FIGURE 8.1 *Service investment value curve*

the high ground is around 2.5 per cent of the original transformation cost per annum, which, in the example of a £1 million programme, would involve the reinvestment of £25,000 per annum in order to keep the service proposition where it needs to be. This level of investment would be used to maintain the value of such items as standards accreditation, the cost of staff and employee opinion surveys and other benchmarking exercises, all of which would need to involve external specialists.

Maintaining the investment is considerably cheaper than allowing any business value that may have been hard to achieve degrade through lack of management support. If investment value degrades at 15 per cent per annum compared with a maintenance cost of 2.5 per cent per annum, a 600 per cent difference, then it is difficult to see how the initial level of investment on service transformation will provide long-term value unless there is an obvious commitment to keeping it going. This aspect should be addressed explicitly in the business case in order to forestall the otherwise inevitable questions about how committed the service delivery team is to transformation from three different quarters – business management, service delivery staff and customers.

Management expectation

Business managers expect that once a certain standard of service has been achieved, it will be maintained at that level regardless of subsequent changes – especially if they have been involved in helping to sponsor the work. Neglecting to maintain the new service proposition will raise concerns about value for money in relation to any claims made during the justification phase; about how stable the service will be once the honeymoon period is over; and whether the commitment to quality will survive management turnover. These concerns are best addressed by ensuring that any commit-ment to service transformation is backed up by external standards oversight, since the risk of losing accreditation should act as an incentive to main-tain the position. As standards themselves are evolving because of changing market needs, keeping a relationship with an accreditation body provides a mechanism to keep up to date with newer releases of standards such as ITIL, ISO/IEC 20000 and ISO 17799 and therefore maintain relevance. Similarly, should service levels start to degrade some time after the transformation initiative ends, business managers will seek reassurances about whether this represents a temporary glitch or a systemic decline. No transformation pro-gramme should base its success criteria on a single year; rather, it should pledge a commitment to sustain its objectives over a minimum of three to five years and for this to be included in management objectives. Ensuring the commitment to maintain standards is enshrined in job descriptions, medium-term plans and the objectives set for each management job will provide reassurance that any shortfall can be attributed to an individual rather than a systemic failure and therefore provides a means by which man-agement confidence can be assured.

Staff expectation

Service delivery staff are notoriously cynical about change initiatives because of the flavour-of-the-month approach that has long been a part of the IT man-agement culture. Although it may be hard to convince them of the need to change and the benefits that such change will bring in the initial business case formulation, it will be even harder to keep them on board once commitment is seen to wane. The same approach towards embedding the transformation into team, role and individual objectives is important to ensuring that staff understand their contribution to the delivery and will counterbalance any management shortfall. It may, however, be staff members who are causing the problem in the first place as a result of losing interest in working hard. This can be addressed readily through personnel practices such as manage-ment by objectives and incentives linked to results achieved, not just hours worked.

Customer expectation

Customers will be the first group to see a decline in standards and raise their concerns in a number of ways, many of which will not be apparent initially to IT as customers will go to business management. If customers have an involvement in the delivery of service, perhaps as a result of committing to a skilling initiative using techniques such as ECDL, then the concern can be mitigated by customers reasserting their needs if the skilling service is no longer available; if the service is still available but the customer no longer has the appetite for it, then service management can escalate the problem. For instances where the customer is a recipient of, rather than a participant in, a service, then a complaints mechanism that should have been set up as part of the transformation programme is an appropriate way in which the customer's concerns can be escalated and addressed.

Continual service improvement

Maintaining the service proposition at the initial levels laid out in the business case is one part of the challenge of maintaining its value. A corresponding objective is to make sure that service standards track the marketplace because in IT, just as much as in any fast-moving market, standards are continually increasing. The essence of continual service improvement is that any standard agreed at the outset will need to be re-examined periodically in order to ensure it is still fit for purpose and that yesterday's service transformation project does not become tomorrow's outsourcing initiative. An obvious way to do this is by periodically benchmarking the KPIs and CSFs used in the management and reporting of service quality and adjusting the targets based on knowledge about latest best practice. Another key method is through the deployment of a service quality improvement (SQI) team using techniques such as Six Sigma, as introduced in Chapter 4, in order to examine areas of potential benefit over and above the initial go-live proposition. In the same way as maintaining the position attracts a cost, so does the process of continual improvement – although a key difference between the two mechanisms is that SQI can be self-financing. Although the cost of SQI is tangible – and it is prudent to budget for about 2.5 per cent per annum of the initial transformation programme expenditure – payback should be seen in a progressive enhancement of that proposition and the delivery of both IT and customer benefits. For an initial £1 million programme cost, £25,000 a year to develop and enhance the service proposition though an SQI approach is not excessive and is, alongside the companion approach of maintenance to keep on the high ground, only one-third of the otherwise inevitable 15 per cent decline per annum in business value.

INDUSTRY AWARDS AND ACCREDITATIONS

Assessing your organization against the industry is an important way of finding out whether the service proposition really is worth investing in. As a means of benchmarking, awards processes are one way of finding out how good you actually are, although they do carry the risk of rejection, which can be demotivating. Industry awards recognize achievement rather than intent to achieve and so, although they can form an important part of the initial plan, they are timed for most appropriately when part of the plan is ready for external validation. Gaining awards or other external recognition from industry bodies with appropriate credentials will not only validate your achievements to management but also offer moral support to the teams undergoing what may well be fundamental change. Trophies, plaques and certificates are also a tangible sign of a serious intent to transform and should be sited in full visibility of everyone, including customers – whether this is in a corporate trophy cupboard, the main reception area or through a website is simply a matter of choice. It is rare to find IT awards displayed among other trophies of corporate recognition, but they do act as a means of communicating to everyone concerned that IT is committed to success in the same way that, say, marketing or premises is and can therefore occupy the same cabinet or wall space. Awards that are felt to be of particular importance are:

- Information Systems Quality at Work (ISQW) accreditation, which shows that the organization has adopted a formal approach to career and skills development for its IT staff;
- the Investors in People award, which accredits the staff development and training schemes against best HR practice;
- industry scheme achievements, such as the Service Excellence and IT Professional Awards, which rank different aspects of IT delivery against a peer group as well as objective minimum standards;
- accreditation against a major standard such as ISO 9000 or ISO/IEC 20000;
- conformance with web usability standards, such as Web Accessibility Initiative (WAI) and PAS78 for website accessibility.

However, awards are of use only if they are seen in the context of being markers on the journey to world class; they are not deliverables in their own right. In fact, there is negative value in accumulating such trophies unless they are part of a wider transformation initiative, because customers will not see the award being reflected in the service they receive.

SUMMARY

- Establish KPIs and CSFs as part of the service transformation justification to act as the quantification for what will be achieved.
- Plan to achieve 15 per cent service quality improvement per annum as a means of assessing how long a transformation initiative should take.
- Assign a change manager to deliver the programme rather than expect one of the current team to do the job alongside their existing role.
- Expect to allocate up to 5 per cent of the programme cost to maintain what has been achieved and to invest in continual service quality improvement.
- Use industry awards and accreditations to maintain awareness of progress against the market and to establish management credibility.

References

Cullum, P. (2006) *The Stupid Company*. National Consumer Council, London.

Voss, C.A., Blackmon, K., Chase, R., Rose, E.L. and Roth, A.V. (1997) Service competitiveness – an Anglo-USA study. *Business Strategy Review* 8, 7–22.

Index

World Class IT Service Delivery

Peter Wheatcroft

A manual on reaching - and sustaining - best practice in terms of performance, delivery and outlook in IT services to avoid customer dissatisfaction. Essential for IT service managers, IT directors, managers and procurement specialists.

ISBN: 978-1-902505-82-4
Price: £25   Size: 246 x 172   Paperback: 192pp
Published: May 2007   www.bcs.org/books/servicedelivery

Business Analysis

Debra Paul and Donald Yeates (Editors)

A practical introductory guide for improving the effectiveness of IT and its alignment with an organisation's business objectives. Covers strategy analysis, modelling business systems/processes, business case development, managing change, requirements engineering and information resource management.

ISBN: 978-1-902505-70-1
Price: £25   Size: 246 x 172mm   Paperback: 256pp
Published: April 2006   www.bcs.org/books/businessanalysis

Finance for IT Decision Makers

A practical handbook for buyers, sellers and managers (2nd Edition)

Michael Blackstaff

This covers aspects of finance relevant to IT professionals who make or influence decisions about IT. Written in plain language with practical examples, it explains: how to construct a financial case for IT projects; financing methods; current standards and legislation; cost/benefit analysis; investment evaluation methods; budgeting, costing and pricing; and more.

ISBN: 978-1-902505-73-2
Price: £30   Size: 246 x 172mm   Paperback: 324pp
Published: July 2006   www.bcs.org/books/finance

Principles of Data Management
Facilitating Information Sharing
Keith Gordon

A practical guide to managing data – an increasingly important asset in all businesses. Invaluable for managing, marketing and IT directors and all business managers.

ISBN: 978-1-902505-84-8
Price: £29.95 Size 246 x 172 Paperback: 274pp
Published: May 2007 www.bcs.org/books/datamanagement

Practical Data Migration
John Morris

Techniques and strategies for ensuring data migration projects achieve maximum return on investment. This practical guide contains: original methods; ideas on rescuing ailing projects; and a model of best practice to be used as a starting point for implementation of the methods. All blended with real life examples and clear definitions of commonly used jargon.

ISBN: 978-1-902505-71-8
Price: £30 Size: 246 x 172mm Paperback: 224pp
Published: May 2006 www.bcs.org/books/datamigration

Global Services
Moving to a Level Playing Field
Mark Kobayashi-Hillary and Dr Richard Sykes

Global Sourcing experts give an overview of how globalisation of the service industry is changing businesses and opening new opportunities to industries. A guide for managing, finance and IT directors and purchasing managers in all industries.

ISBN: 978-1-902505-83-1
Price: £25 Size: 246 x 172 Paperback: 192pp
Published: April 2007 www.bcs.org/books/globalservices

A Guide to Global Sourcing
Offshore outsourcing and other global delivery models

Elizabeth Anne Sparrow

The opportunities and obstacles associated with offshore outsourcing and other global delivery models.
Country-by-country analysis of offshore services available.

ISBN: 978-1-902505-61-9
Price: £25 Size: 246 x 172mm Paperback: 196pp
Published: November 2004 www.bcs.org/books/globalsourcing

Invisible Architecture
The benefits of aligning people, processes and technology

Jenny Ure & Gudrun Jaegersberg

The biggest problems faced in implementing computer systems, especially across different countries, are often not technical – they are 'socio-technical'. *Invisible Architecture* uses real examples to highlight the potential for harnessing 'soft' factors to competitive advantage.

ISBN: 978-1-902505-59-6
Price: £25 Size: 246 x 172mm Paperback: 104pp
Published: March 2005 www.bcs.org/books/invisiblearchitecture

Software Testing An ISEB Foundation
Brian Hambling (Editor) Peter Morgan,
Geoff Thompson, Angelina Samaroo, Peter Williams

Providing a practical insight into the world of software testing, this book explains the basic steps of the testing process and how to perform effective tests. It supports the revised 'ISEB Foundation Certificate in Software Testing' and includes self-assessment exercises, worked examples and sample exam questions.

ISBN: 978-1-902505-79-4
Price: £20 Size: 246 x 172mm Paperback: 220pp
Published: September 2006 www.bcs.org/books/softwaretesting

Project Management in The Real World
Shortcuts to success
Elizabeth Harrin

Project Management in the Real World is a short cut to project management experience: it summarizes over 250 years of expertise from experienced project managers. It offers hints and tips on controlling budget, time, scope and people; managing project budgets; managing project scope; managing project teams; managing project plans; and managing yourself.

ISBN: 978-1-902505-81-7
Price: £20 Size: 246 x 172mm Paperback: 225pp
Published: November 2006 www.bcs.org/books/realworldPM

Project Management for IT-Related Projects
Textbook for the ISEB Foundation Certificate in IS Project Management
Bob Hughes (Editor), Roger Ireland, Brian West, Norman Smith and David I. Shepherd

The principles of IT-related project management, including project planning, monitoring and control, change management, risk management and communication between project stakeholders. Encompasses the entire syllabus of the 'ISEB Foundation Certificate in IS Project Management'.

ISBN: 978-1-902505-58-9
Price: £20 Size: 297 x 210mm Paperback: 148pp
Published: August 2004 www.bcs.org/books/projectmanagement

Business Process Management
A Rigorous Approach
Martyn A. Ould

A rigorous way of understanding the mass of concurrent, collaborative activity that goes on within an organisation, giving a solid basis for developing IT systems that actually support a business's processes.

ISBN: 978-1-902505-60-2
Price: £35 Size: 246 x 172mm Paperback: 364pp
Published: January 2005 www.bcs.org/books/bpm

A Pragmatic Guide to
Business Process Modelling

Jon Holt

Explores all aspects of process modelling from process analysis to process documentation by applying a standard modelling notation, UML. Guidance for directors and managers on business process modelling to improve processes, productivity and profitability.

ISBN: 978-1-902505-66-4
Price: £30 Size: 246 x 172mm Paperback: 184pp
Published: Sept 2005 www.bcs.org/books/processmodelling

Data Protection & Compliance in Context

Stewart Room

This pragmatic guide explains the data protection laws; provides practical advice on protecting data privacy under the Data Protection Act, human rights laws and freedom of information legislation; and gives a platform for building compliance strategies. The author, Stewart Room, is the chair of the National Association of Data Protection and Freedom of Information Officers (NADPO).

ISBN: 978-1-902505-78-7
Price: £35 Size: 246 x 172mm Paperback: 304pp
Published: Oct 2006 www.bcs.org/books/dataprotection

A Managers Guide to IT Law

Jeremy Newton and Jeremy Holt (Editors)

This comprehensive guide to the IT-related legal issues explains, in plain English, the most relevant legal frameworks, with examples from actual case law used to illustrate the kinds of problems and disputes that most commonly arise. Contents include: IT contracts; systems procurement contracts; avoiding employment problems; instructing an IT consultant; intellectual property law; escrow; outsourcing; data protection.

ISBN: 978-1-902505-55-8
Price: £25 Size: 246 x 172mm Paperback: 180pp
Published: July 2004 www.bcs.org/books/itlaw

Professional Issues in Information Technology

Frank Bott

This book explores the relationship between technological change, society and the law, and the powerful role that computers and computer professionals play in a technological society. Designed to accompany the BCS Professional Examination core Diploma module: 'Professional Issues in Information Systems Practice'.

ISBN: 978-1-902505-65-7
Price: £20 Size: 246 x 172mm Paperback: 248pp
Published: May 2005 www.bcs.org/books/professionalissues

Forthcoming Titles

Look out for forthcoming titles on the following subjects:

Digital Rights Management
IT Procurement
Business Focussed IT
Information Security Management
eBusiness Strategy
IT Enabled Business Change

and a range of IT Service Management books.

About the Publisher

The British Computer Society (BCS) is the leading professional body for the IT industry. BCS leads the IT industry in professionalism, accreditation and examinations. 50 years old in 2007 and with members in over 100 countries, BCS is the professional and learned society in the field of computers and information technology. BCS publishes books, magazines and journals for members and other IT professionals.

Call for Authors

The BCS would welcome proposals from potential authors for books at the business/IT interface. If you are interested in writing a book for the BCS please visit: www.bcs.org/books/writer for more information or contact Matthew Flynn by emailing him at: matthew.flynn@hq.bcs.org.uk

BCS ORDER FORM

To order your book(s), please complete this form and send it to:
BCS Books, York Publishing Services, 64 Hallfield Road, Layerthorpe, York, YO31 7ZQ.
Fax: +44 (0)1904 430 868. Enquiries to: orders@yps-publishing.co.uk.
BCS Books are also available in all good bookshops.

	Price	Qty	BCS Member Price	Qty
World Class IT Service Delivery	£25		£20	
Business Analysis	£25		£20	
Finance for IT Decision Makers	£30		£25	
Principles of Data Management	£29.95		£25	
Practical Data Migration	£30		£25	
Global Services: Moving to a Level Playing Field	£25		£20	
A Guide To Global Sourcing	£25		£20	
Invisible Architecture	£25		£20	
Software Testing	£20		£15	
Project Management in the Real World	£20		£15	
Project Management for IT-Related Projects	£20		£15	
Business Process Management	£35		£30	
A Pragmatic Guide to Business Process Modelling	£30		£25	
Data Protection and Compliance in Context	£35		£30	
A Manager's Guide to IT Law	£25		£20	
Professional Issues in Information Technology	£20		£15	

P&P: UK £2.75 for the first book, plus 75p for any additional items.
Europe £5. Rest of world £12.

Postage: £ [   ]
Total: £ [   ]

Title: .... Initials: .... Surname: ....

Delivery address: ....

Telephone: .... Email: ....

BCS membership number (if applicable): ....

I enclose a cheque ☐ made payable to '**The British Computer Society**' or please charge my:

☐ **Visa** ☐ **Mastercard** ☐ **Switch** ☐ **Maestro** (please indicate) We are unable to accept American Express

Start date (Maestro/Switch only): .... Issue number (Maestro/Switch only): ....

Expiry date: .... Card number: ....

Name as it appears on card: ....

Card holder's address (if diffrent from delivery address): ....
....

Signature: ....

*Please note: To protect you from fraud we now require the security number on your credit card when making payment. For most cards it is the last 3 digits on the back of the card. If you would rather not write your security number on this form you can call us on +44 (0)1904 431 218 to place this order. Once your order has been processed the record of your security number will be destoyed.

Please note: Information is correct at the time of going to press. However it is subject to change without notice.

...rity Number